Stained Glass
Quilts
Made Easy

AMY WHALEN HELMKAMP

CREDITS

President . . . . Nancy J. Martin
CEO . . . . Daniel J. Martin
Publisher . . . . Jane Hamada
Editorial Director . . . . . . Mary V. Green
Editorial Project Manager . . . . Tina Cook
Design and Production
    Manager . . . . Stan Green
Technical Editor . . . . Karen Soltys
Copy Editor . . . . Ellen Balstad
Illustrators . . . . Laurel Strand
                and Lisa McKenney
Photographer . . . . Brent Kane
Cover Designer . . . . Magrit Baurecht
Text Designer . . . . Trina Stahl

Martingale
& C O M P A N Y

That
Patchwork
Place®

That Patchwork Place is an imprint of
Martingale & Company.

Stained Glass Quilts Made Easy
© 2000 by Amy Whalen Helmkamp

Martingale & Company
20205 144th Ave NE
Woodinville, WA 98072-8478 USA
www.martingale-pub.com

Printed in China
05 04 03 02 01   6 5 4 3 2

MISSION STATEMENT

We are dedicated to providing quality
products and service
by working together to inspire
creativity and to enrich
the lives we touch.

Library of Congress Cataloging-in-
Publication Data

Helmkamp, Amy.
    Stained glass quilts made easy / Amy
Helmkamp.
        p.   cm.
    ISBN 1-56477-319-1
    1. Patchwork—Patterns. 2. Quilting—
Patterns. 3. Appliqué—Patterns. I. Title.

TT835.H442 2000
746.46'041—dc21

                                00-032861

Contents

FOR MANY YEARS, I admired stained glass quilts and wanted to make one. Unfortunately, I did not have the time to create one of these beautiful quilts by using the standard method of construction, which required applying yards of bias tape over the edges of the appliqué pieces.

I began searching through books and on the Internet for alternative ways to construct stained glass quilts, but I couldn't find a technique that satisfied my need to create a stained glass quilt quickly and easily. So, I devised my own method to meet my requirements and called it "Sew Easy Stained Glass." Using fusible web and no bias tape, I created a beautiful stained glass quilt in a fraction of the time of the traditional technique. By fusing the pattern pieces to a background of solid black fabric and leaving a ¼" space between all of the pieces, I created the look of *leading,* which is a term for the lead bars that hold real pieces of stained glass together. I achieved the look of a stained glass quilt without all of the work!

I approached shop owners in my neighborhood with my stained glass quilt samples in hand and was thrilled to receive their approval. They even encouraged me to develop patterns to sell, and the rest, as they say, is history.

Now it's your turn to try my method in *Stained Glass Quilts Made Easy.* You'll be surprised at just how quick and easy my technique is. You can have your first project ready to hang on the wall in just a few hours, which will leave you with plenty of time to come back for more!

Amy

STAINED GLASS WINDOWS have been in existence for more than a thousand years. I do not know the point at which the look of stained glass was applied to quilt tops, but I do know that making a stained glass quilt is a fascinating, fun, and totally different process than sewing a more traditional pieced quilt.

In this book, I cover everything you'll need to know to create your own stained glass quilts. You'll find directions for preparing your patterns and the foundation fabric, directions for machine quilting and binding, and even brief instructions for using other stained glass quilting methods.

Once you review the techniques, try them out with one of the twelve quilt projects featured in the book. Patterns and step-by-step directions for these twelve quilts are provided. You can use the patterns as they're printed, or modify them and add your own ideas. I guarantee that once you try one of the projects, you'll have so much fun you'll be anxious to try another. And with so many fabrics to choose from and so many colors available, each quilt will be unique and have a character all its own. You can even use the patterns for other craft methods, such as garment appliqué, painting on wood, or woodcarving. Give your imagination free rein and see where it leads you.

Techniques

What You'll Need

It's important to have the right type of supplies on hand before you start your stained glass quilt so that you won't have to search your sewing room or make a late-night jaunt to the quilt shop while in the middle of your project.

Fabrics

Choose good-quality fabrics for making your stained glass quilt. I prefer to use 100 percent cotton fabrics. You may choose to try fabrics of varying fiber contents. If so, please test these fabrics first to see how well they work with your fusible web. I like to use batiks and hand-dyed fabrics because their subtle shadings most closely simulate true stained glass. But don't limit yourself. These quilts look equally beautiful made from fabrics with a print design on them. Don't be afraid to experiment to find the look that you like best.

TIP: If you like the color of a fabric but the print seems a bit too bold to use in your stained glass project, take a look at the wrong side of the fabric. Often the color will be the same but the print will be much more subdued.

For your quilt foundation fabric, you will use a solid black fabric. If you choose very pale fabrics for your appliqué pieces, you may find that the black "shadows" through the fabrics. Make a small test sample to see if the show-through is undesirable. Usually the added layer of fusible web prevents show-through, but test first to be sure.

Always wash and iron your fabrics before you begin. Some fabrics contain a finish that may interfere with your fusible web's ability to do its job.

Fusible Web

There are a number of fusible webs on the market, and though all are suitable for my "Sew Easy Stained Glass" method, I recommend Steam-a-Seam 2. It has a double-stick surface that temporarily holds the appliqué pieces in place. You can stick—but not fuse—all the pieces in place, peel them off, and move them around until you are satisfied with how your quilt top looks. The sticky surface holds the pieces in place while you fuse them, too. I also find that the edges of the appliqué pieces do not need to be stitched down like you need to do with other fusible webs. You only need to use a straight stitch to do the outline quilting around the appliqué pieces rather than a securing stitch of some type around each piece.

Monofilament and Cotton Thread

Depending on the type of fusible web you use, you may or may not want to stitch the appliqué edges in place after fusing. If you use a lightweight or sewable web, I advise stitching over the edges of the appliqué pieces with a monofilament thread to keep them firmly in place. When shopping for supplies, be sure to pick up a spool of .004 monofilament thread. I recommend Sulky's monofilament thread. It is made from polyester and is very soft. You'll also need basic black cotton thread for your bobbin. If you use heavyweight or non-sewable fusible web, don't try to stitch the edges in place. Simply use black cotton thread both in the needle and in the bobbin for quilting your finished project.

TIP: Monofilament thread comes in two colors: clear and smoke. Since the majority of your stitching will be on black fabric, you may choose to use the smoke thread. The clear thread, even though it is "invisible," reflects more light than the smoke thread. This makes the clear thread sparkle, and it may stand out more than you want. I use the clear monofilament, but the choice is yours.

Other Supplies

There are just a few other basic supplies that you'll need to make any of the projects in this book: a rotary cutter and mat, a rotary-cutting ruler, craft scissors, an iron and ironing board, a pencil, and a permanent marker such as a fine-point Sharpie.

If, after reading through the directions, you decide that you'd prefer to trace your entire pattern onto the foundation fabric rather than just using outer guidelines, you may also want to purchase tracing paper that is made for transferring marks to fabric. You can find this in any sewing shop. Saral brand is one I like because it makes a distinct mark when you trace over it, yet it's chalky so it brushes off easily. It doesn't leave an oily residue like some types may.

If you have a light box, it may come in handy. However, if you use either tracing paper or the guideline methods that I explain on the following pages, you really won't need one.

APPLIQUÉ PREPARATION

Tracing the Design onto Fusible Web

Note that each pattern is the mirror image of how your finished quilt will look. If you don't want the finished design to be reversed, trace the design onto your fusible web from the backside of the pattern. You may find that using a light table or taping the pattern up against a window will make this job easier.

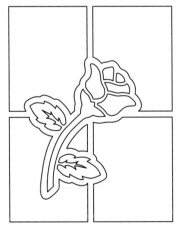

Pattern design

Also note that most of the project patterns in this book are printed on more than one page. To trace

each pattern accurately, you'll need to have a complete, assembled copy of the pattern. Copy the separate pages and join them as indicated on the pattern to create your full-size pattern.

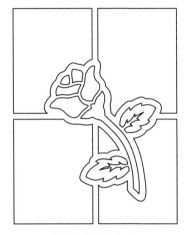

Finished quilt design

From the quilt pattern, trace the pattern pieces onto the paper backing side of the fusible web with a pencil or a permanent marking pen. Trace the pattern pieces in groups—all background pieces together, all leaves and stems together, and so on—so that you can press them to their corresponding fabrics without cutting all the small pieces apart. Be sure to copy the pattern number onto your fusible web.

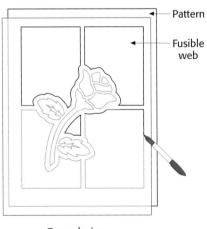

Trace design.

Fusing the Appliqué Pieces

Press all fabrics. Next, following the manufacturer's instructions, fuse the web pieces to the appliqué fabrics you have chosen. Cut out the appliqué pieces exactly on your drawn lines and set them aside.

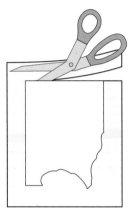

Cut out pieces.

FOUNDATION PREPARATION

THE FOUNDATION is the black fabric to which you will apply your appliqué pieces. Before you can appliqué, you'll need to prepare the foundation. First, from black fabric, cut out your foundation according to the dimensions given in the project directions.

Next, you will need to mark your foundation fabric in preparation for placing the appliqué pieces. I've described three different methods that you can use. You may want to try out each one to see what you like best or pick a method based on what tools or supplies you have.

Method One—Guidelines

1. Using a rotary-cutting ruler and a light-colored pencil, mark a guideline 2" in from each side of the foundation fabric.

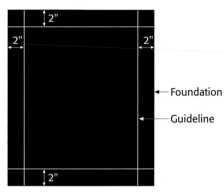

Draw guidelines.

2. Referring to the appliqué guide for your project, place your appliqué pieces on the foundation. Work inward from the guidelines. Be sure you leave the same amount of space between each appliqué piece. You should have ¼" of black leading showing between all the appliqué pieces unless otherwise stated in the project directions.

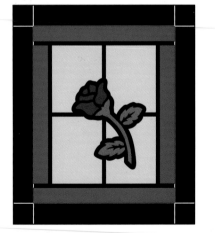

Place pieces.

Method Two—Tracing Paper

1. Use tracing paper that is meant for tracing and transferring marks to fabric. With this kind of paper, one side is coated so that you leave a mark on the fabric when you draw over the pattern lines.

2. To transfer the design onto the black foundation fabric, place the tracing paper—colored-side down—on the right side of the fabric. Lay the pattern on top of the layers so that it is facing in the opposite direction from how you traced your appliqué pieces. Center it over the foundation fabric. Trace all lines of the pattern with a dull pencil. If the pencil is too sharp, it will tear through the pattern and tracing paper.

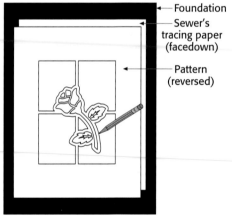

—⟨ ⟩—

TIP: Tracing just inside each piece allows you to cover up your marks when the appliqué pieces are placed on the foundation fabric. You won't have to worry about removing any marks after you finish fusing the pieces in place.

Method Three—Light Box

1. Use a light source such as a light box or window to help you place your pattern pieces. Tape the quilt pattern onto the lightbox or the window so that it is facing in the opposite direction from how you traced your appliqué pieces.

2. Lay the foundation fabric over the pattern, and either trace the pattern onto the fabric with a light-colored marking pencil or use the pattern lines that show through to help you position the appliqué pieces directly on the foundation fabric. Make sure that the center of the pattern is matched with the center of the foundation fabric.

NOTE: *If you aren't using Steam-A-Seam 2 that temporarily sticks to the fabric, trace the lines first if you use a window as your light source. Other fusible webs won't stay in place when you position them on a vertical surface.*

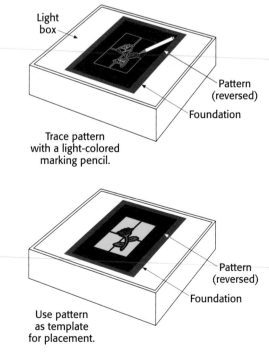

Trace pattern with a light-colored marking pencil.

Use pattern as template for placement.

ATTACHING THE APPLIQUÉS

Using the printed pattern as a reference, begin placing the appliqué pieces onto the foundation fabric. Leave a ¼" space between all of the pieces unless otherwise specified in the project directions. These spaces represent the stained glass leading. If you are using the guideline method, which is method one, begin by placing the border pieces on first and work your way inward to the center of the quilt pattern. You may use a ruler to check your spacing if you desire. If you are using the tracing methods (methods two or three), place your appliqué pieces on first and then add the border pieces.

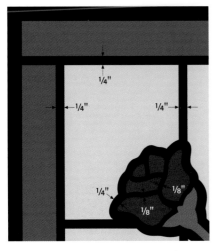

Place pieces, beginning with borders.

Continue placing pieces until the design is complete. Once you have placed all of the pieces, study your top for a few moments. Are you satisfied with how it looks? If not, now is the time to adjust the placement of your pieces—or change the color of a piece if it's not working as well as you originally thought it would.

TIP: If you are not using a double-stick fusible web, you will need to place your foundation on a large, flat surface, such as a board covered by a folded bed sheet that you can carry to your ironing board for the fusing process.

Once you are happy with how the design looks, fuse your appliqué pieces in place following the manufacturer's instructions that came with the fusible web. Be sure not to press for longer than the recommended time. Too much heat can result in poor bonding of the appliqué piece to the foundation. Sometimes the glue of the fusible web can even seep through to the right side of the appliqué piece.

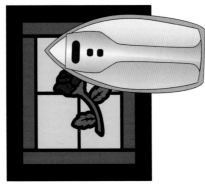

Fuse appliqué pieces.

QUILTING AND FINISHING

After your quilt top has cooled, you're ready to layer, baste, and quilt it, just as you would for any other type of quilt.

Basting

Cut your quilt backing and batting according to the dimensions given in the project directions. Place your backing fabric right side down on the floor or table. Next, place the batting and finally the quilt top, right side up, on top. Baste the layers together in the leading areas (the black foundation fabric area between the appliqué pieces). You can use safety pins, a needle and white thread, or a quilt tacking system.

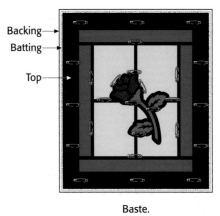

Baste.

TIP: You may also use one of the new basting sprays to hold the layers together while quilting. Since these projects are small, the basting spray will easily hold the layers together securely throughout your entire quilting process. To use, follow the directions on the basting spray can.

Machine Quilting

The type of quilting stitch I use on my stained glass quilts depends upon the type of fusible web I use.

———————⌇———————

TIP: If you have an open-toe embroidery foot, you will find it very helpful when quilting. This style of foot allows for better visibility when quilting around the appliqué pieces.

Lightweight Fusible Web

If you used a lightweight fusible web for your appliqué, choose one of the following machine stitches to secure the edges of your appliqué pieces:

Long, narrow zigzag stitch

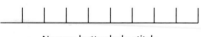

Narrow buttonhole stitch

– – – ⋀ – – – ⋀ – – – ⋀ – – – ⋀ – – – ⋀

Blind hem stitch

With .004 invisible monofilament thread on top and thread to match your backing fabric in the bobbin, stitch around each appliqué piece. You will be sewing down the edges of the appliqué pieces and quilting your quilt at the same time.

NOTE: *You may need to adjust the tension on your sewing machine to accommodate the monofilament thread. It is very lightweight, and you won't want the bobbin thread pulling up to the top of your quilt. Test sew on fabric scraps to see if you will need to tighten or loosen your upper tension.*

Heavy-Duty Fusible Web

If you used a heavy-duty or no-sew fusible web for your appliqués, use black thread and a straight stitch to quilt around the outside edges of the appliqué pieces. Don't stitch through the appliqués or the heavy-duty layer of fusible web may gum up your needle after just a few stitches. Read the manufacturer's instructions that come with your fusible web.

Attaching the Binding

After you complete the quilting, you will need to trim away the excess foundation fabric, batting, and backing fabric from each side of the quilt before adding the binding. Lay the completed quilt on your cutting mat, and measure ½" away from the outside edges of the border pieces with your rotary-cutting ruler. (Once the binding is attached, you'll have ½" of leading, including the binding, showing around the entire quilt top.) Use your rotary cutter to trim off the excess fabric and batting.

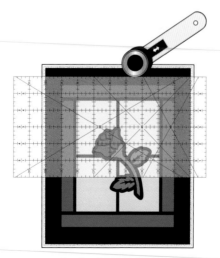

Trim, leaving ½" all around
the outside edges of the border pieces.

1. Cut the binding strips according to the project directions. These strips are cut along the crosswise length of the fabric (selvage to selvage). With right sides facing each other, place the ends of two strips together to form a right angle as shown. Stitch the diagonal seam as shown. Trim ¼" from this seam and press the seam allowance open. Repeat for all strips to form one long continuous strip.

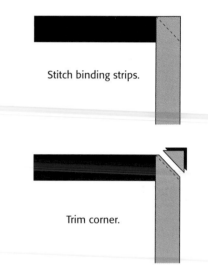

Stitch binding strips.

Trim corner.

2. Fold the completed binding strip in half lengthwise, with *wrong* sides together, and press. With the right side of the quilt top facing up, place one end of the binding near the center of one side of the quilt. Make sure to align the raw edges of the binding with the raw edges of the quilt top; pin in place. Using a ¼" seam allowance, begin stitching close to the corner.

Begin stitching 2" from edge.

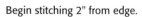

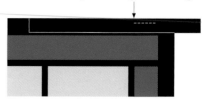

3. Stitch to within ¼" of the corner. Stop with the needle in the down position, raise the presser foot, turn the quilt a quarter turn, and backstitch off the edge of the quilt.

Turn and backstitch off quilt.

4. Raise the presser foot and remove the quilt from the machine. Flip the binding up so that it is parallel with the next side to be stitched as shown.

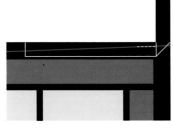

Flip binding strip up.

5. Flip the binding back down so that the folded edge is even with the edge of the quilt. Begin stitching, and stitch until the needle is ¼" from the next corner. Repeat the same process at each corner for perfectly mitered binding corners.

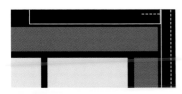

Flip binding down and continue sewing.

6. After turning the last corner, stitch about 1" more of the binding. Remove the quilt from beneath the presser foot. Overlap the ends of the binding. Measure and trim off the excess so that you are left with 2¼" overlapping.

Overlap ends 2¼".

7. Open the two ends of the binding strip. With right sides together, join the ends with the same method described in step 1 that was used to sew the binding strips together. Don't forget to trim away the excess fabric from the seam allowance.

Stitch binding strips.

Trim corner.

8. Finger press the seam allowance open; then refold the binding strip and finish sewing it to the edge of the quilt.

Wrap the binding around to the backside of the quilt, encasing the seam allowance, and pin the binding in place. At each corner, fold the binding on the back to form a mitered corner. On the front, stitch in the ditch around the binding, removing pins as you go. This will attach your binding on the backside while adding a row of quilting on the front. As an alternative, you can stitch the binding down on the back of the quilt by hand using a blind stitch or whipstitch.

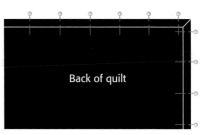

Turn binding to back and pin.

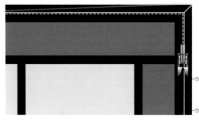

Stitch in the ditch on the right side of the quilt.

TIP: If you have an edgestitch foot for your machine, use it when stitching in the ditch. An edgestitch foot opens up the seam for closer stitching.

Making a Hanging Sleeve

To display your quilt, you'll want to add a hanging sleeve. Take the strip that you cut for the hanging sleeve (as called for in the project directions), and sew a narrow hem on each short end. Fold the strip in half lengthwise, right sides together, and sew a ¼" seam. Turn the sleeve right side out.

Position the sleeve on the back of the quilt with the *bottom* edge of the sleeve 2½" down from the top edge of the quilt. Whipstitch the sleeve to the quilt backing only, along both long edges. Place a dowel that is 2" longer than the sleeve into the sleeve. Hang your quilt from the ends of the dowel, or attach a decorative cord to the dowel ends and hang the quilt from the cord.

2½"
Back of quilt

Banners

If you'd like to hang your quilt top as a banner rather than as a quilt, use these finishing directions. For a banner, there is only one layer—no batting or quilt backing—and no quilt binding.

1. After the quilt top is completely fused but not quilted, measure and cut away 1" from the outside edges of the *side and bottom edges only. Do not* trim any fabric from the top edge.

2. Finish all four edges with a ¼" double-folded hem. To make this hem, turn under ¼" on all four sides of the quilt and press. Then turn under another ¼" on all the edges and topstitch the narrow hem in place.

3. On the top edge, create a casing by turning down 1" and stitching close to the edge of the hemmed edge.

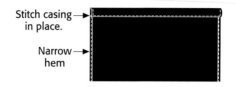

Stitch casing in place.

Narrow hem

4. Slide a dowel through the casing, add a hanging cord, and your banner is complete.

Making a Label

Always be sure to create a label for your quilt that includes information about your quilt, such as who made the quilt, when it was made, and any other facts you would like to record. This will provide future admirers of your quilt with historical facts about it.

You can make a label from one of the light-colored fabrics in your quilt top by writing the information on it with a Pigma pen or embroidering it. You can hand stitch the label to the back of your quilt, or you can fuse it in place with left-over fusible web. If you're feeling really creative, you can even adapt part of the quilt top design and make a miniature version to dress up your label with appliqué.

OPTIONAL METHODS OF CONSTRUCTION

I F YOU PREFER not to use fusible web in your quilt top, there are other ways to use my stained glass patterns. Choose the method that suits you best!

Hand or Machine Appliqué

If you like to appliqué by hand, you can construct any of the quilts in this book by using hand appliqué instead of the fusible web. Simply trace the pattern pieces onto freezer paper, press the freezer paper templates onto your appliqué fabrics, and cut out the fabric shapes, adding a ¼" seam allowance all around. Press the seam allowance to the back of the appliqué piece or baste the seam allowance in place.

Position the pieces on the foundation fabric following the placement guide, and baste or pin them in place. Then stitch the appliqués in place with a blindstitch, ladder stitch, or your favorite stitch. Remove the freezer paper before completing the final stitches on each piece.

You can also attach freezer paper appliqué shapes to your quilt top using machine appliqué. Refer to page 10 for the various stitches that you can use. As with hand appliqué, you'll need to remove the freezer paper before the entire piece has been attached.

Traditional Stained Glass Method

You may also opt to construct any of the quilt projects by using the traditional method for making stained glass quilts. The steps for this method are listed below.

1. Make a plastic template for each appliqué piece in the quilt. Trace around the templates onto your appliqué fabrics.

2. Cut out the appliqué pieces, adding ⅛" around the marked lines as you cut.

3. Place the appliqués on a foundation fabric such as muslin, and baste them in place, butting the edges of the pieces together. Using purchased bias tape or bias tape that you made, cover the edges of the appliqué pieces. Center the bias tape over the line created by the butted pieces.

4. Hand sew the edges of the bias tape in place, or use a machine straight stitch to sew them in place. For an alternative sewing method, see step 5.

5. With the bias-tape method, you can stitch the bias tape in place while quilting, which allows you to make the project more quickly and easily. Before positioning the bias tape, layer the backing, batting, and quilt top together, and baste. Next, position the bias tape as described in step 3. Using one of the machine stitches shown in the illustration on page 10, sew along the edges of the bias tape. You'll attach the bias tape and quilt your project all at the same time.

———— ✐ ————

TIP: For this last method, you may choose to use the new fusible bias tape that is on the market.

Posies

Posies by Amy Whalen Helmkamp, 1999,
Lake Oswego, Oregon, 12" x 15".

*Simple and innocent, posies bring to mind the handfuls
of flowers my daughters would bring to me when
they were young.*

MATERIALS

*All fabrics are 42" wide and 100
percent cotton unless otherwise stated.*

- ¾ yd. black solid fabric for
  foundation, backing, binding,
  and hanging sleeve
- ⅛ yd. or 5" x 12" rectangle of
  mottled purple fabric for border
  strips
- 12" square of mottled cream
  fabric for background pieces 1–11
- 6" square of mottled green
  fabric for stem and leaf
  pieces 12–20
- 3½" square each of mottled red,
  yellow, and blue fabrics for posy
  pieces 21–23
- 1" x 3" piece of bright gold print
  for posy center pieces 21a, 22a,
  and 23a
- ⅔ yd. fusible web
- 15" x 18" piece of batting
- Black cotton thread for no-sew
  fusible web, plus monofilament
  thread if you use lightweight
  fusible web

CUTTING

From the black solid fabric:

1. Cut 2 strips, each 2½" x 42", for
   the binding. Set them aside.

2. Cut a 4½" x 11½" rectangle for
   the hanging sleeve. Set it aside.

3. Cut 2 pieces, each 15" x 18", for
   the foundation and the quilt
   backing. Set them aside.

PREPARING THE APPLIQUÉS

NOTE: *The pattern is the mirror image of your finished quilt. Should you wish to have the finished design face the same direction as the pattern, turn the pattern over and trace the pieces from the backside of the pattern.*

1. Draw the border pieces onto the fusible web. Using a ruler, draw two 1" x 11" strips and two 1" x 11½" strips. The 1" x 11½" strips will be the side borders, and the 1" x 11" strips will be the top and bottom borders.

2. Referring to "Tracing the Design onto Fusible Web" on page 7, trace the pattern pieces on pages 16–17 onto the fusible web. Group pieces together that will be cut from the same fabric. For instance, all of the background pieces (1–11) are cut from the mottled cream fabric, so trace them close together on one section of your fusible web. Likewise, group the posy center pieces (21a–23a) together, and so on. Write the corresponding pattern number on each piece.

3. After you trace all of the pieces, cut the groups apart and fuse them to the wrong side of the appliqué fabrics. Be sure to refer to the manufacturer's instructions for using the fusible web. Cut out each shape, and set the appliqués aside.

ASSEMBLING THE QUILT TOP

1. Using a ruler and a marking pencil, measure 2" in from each edge of the foundation fabric and draw a line the full length of each side to use as guidelines. Or see page 8 if you prefer to trace your entire pattern onto the foundation fabric.

2. Referring to the appliqué guide below and the pattern, place the appliqué pieces onto the foundation fabric. Begin with the border strips. Place the top and bottom border strips on first, laying the outside edge of each strip on the drawn line. Next, place the side border strips with their outside edges on the drawn lines. Leave a ¼" gap between the ends of these strips and the edges of the top and bottom strips. Use a ruler to check your spacing if you desire.

Appliqué Guide

3. Continuing to work from the outside edges toward the quilt center, place the remaining appliqué pieces onto the foundation fabric. Leave a ¼" gap between all of the pieces.

NOTE: *The posy centers are the exception to this rule. Leave only a ¹⁄₁₆" gap between the flower centers and the petals.*

4. Once you have all of the pieces in place, stand back and study your quilt top. Make any necessary adjustments. Following the manufacturer's directions for your fusible web, press all of the pieces to adhere them to the foundation. Allow the quilt top to cool.

FINISHING

Refer to "Quilting and Finishing" starting on page 9 to complete your quilt or "Banners" on page 12 to turn your quilt top into a banner.

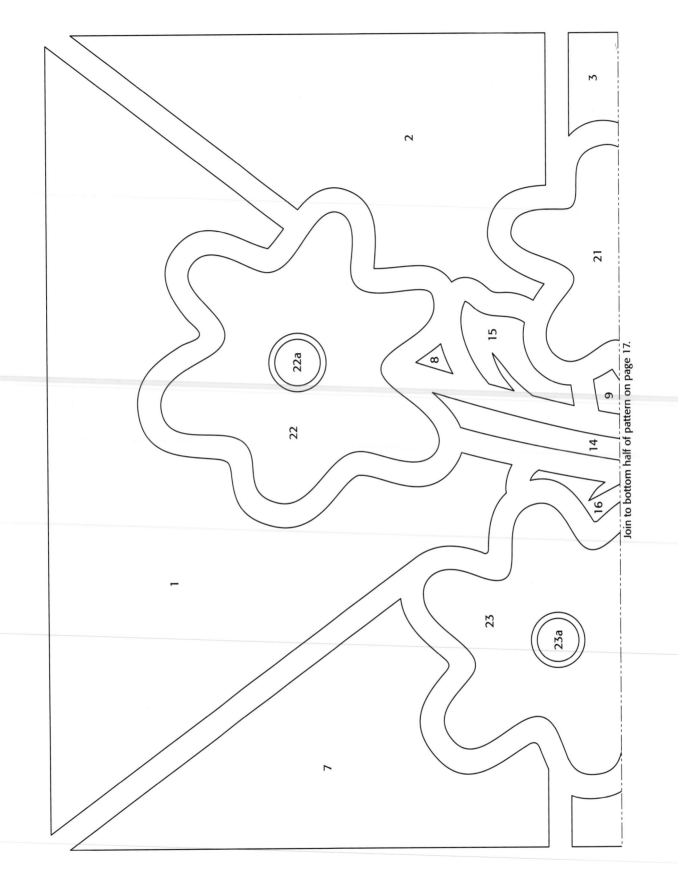

Join to bottom half of pattern on page 17.

Posies
Top Half

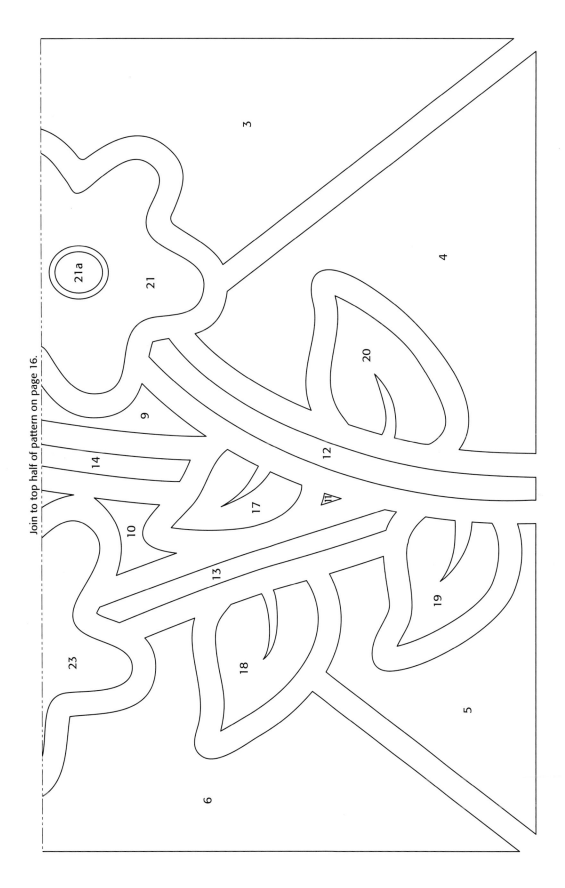

Join to top half of pattern on page 16.

Posies
Bottom Half

Sailing

Sailing by Amy Whalen Helmkamp, 1999,
Lake Oswego, Oregon. 14½" x 18½".

Sailing is a relaxing way to spend the day—smelling the salty sea air, feeling the sun warm your face, listening to the sounds of the waves splashing against the hull of the boat, and hearing the cry of the lonesome sea gull flying overhead.

MATERIALS

All fabrics are 42" wide and 100 percent cotton unless otherwise stated.

- ⅞ yd. black solid fabric for foundation, backing, binding, and hanging sleeve
- ⅛ yd. mottled turquoise and blue fabric for borders
- 12" square of mottled light blue fabric for sky pieces 1–7
- 5" x 7" rectangle white print fabric for cloud pieces 8–10
- 2" square of mottled red print fabric for flag piece 11
- 1" x 7" rectangle of mottled brown fabric for mast piece 12
- 7" square of white fabric for sail pieces 13–15
- 1" x 6" rectangle for sail strip piece 16
- 1" x 5" rectangle of mottled blue fabric for sail strip piece 17
- 3" x 9" rectangle of mottled teal fabric for boat piece 18
- 5" x 16" rectangle of mottled dark blue fabric for water pieces 19–25
- 2" square for sea gull piece 26
- ⅞ yd. fusible web
- 17½" x 21½" piece of batting
- Black cotton thread for no-sew fusible web, plus monofilament thread if you use lightweight fusible web

CUTTING LIST FOR BLACK SOLID FABRIC

From the black solid fabric:

1. Cut 2 strips, each 2½" x 42", for the binding. Set them aside.

2. Cut a 4½" x 18" rectangle for the hanging sleeve. Set it aside.

3. Cut 2 pieces, each 17½" x 21½", for the foundation and the quilt backing. Set them aside.

PREPARING THE APPLIQUÉS

NOTE: *The pattern is the mirror image of your finished quilt. Should you wish to have the finished design face the same direction as the pattern, turn the pattern over and trace the pieces from the backside of the pattern.*

1. Draw the border pieces onto the fusible web. Using a ruler, draw two 1" x 11" strips and two 1" x 17½" strips. The 1" x 11" strips will be the side borders, and the 1" x 17½" strips will be the top and bottom borders.

2. Referring to "Tracing the Design onto Fusible Web" on page 7, trace the pattern pieces on pages 20–23 onto the fusible web. Group pieces together that will be cut from the same fabric. For instance, all of the sky pieces (1–7) are cut from the blue fabric, so trace them close together on one section of your fusible web. Likewise, group all of the water pieces (19–25) together, and so on. Write the corresponding pattern number on each traced piece.

3. After you trace all of the pieces, cut the groups apart and fuse them to the wrong side of the appliqué fabrics. Be sure to refer to the manufacturer's instructions for using the fusible web. Cut out each shape, and set the appliqués aside.

ASSEMBLING THE QUILT TOP

1. Using a ruler and a marking pencil, measure 2" in from each edge of the foundation fabric and draw a line the full length of each side to use as guidelines. Or see page 8 if you prefer to trace your entire pattern onto the foundation fabric.

2. Referring to the appliqué guide at right and the pattern, place the appliqué pieces onto the foundation fabric. Begin with the border strips. Place the top and bottom border strips on first, laying the outside edge of each strip on the drawn line. Next, place the side border strips with their outside edges on the drawn lines. Leave a ¼" gap between the ends of these strips and the edges of the top and bottom strips. Use a ruler to check your spacing if you desire.

Appliqué Guide

3. Continuing to work from the outside edges toward the quilt center, place the remaining appliqué pieces onto the foundation fabric. Leave a ¼" gap between each piece.

NOTE: *The sea gull and the stripes in the sail are an exception to this rule. Leave only a ⅛" gap around the sea gull and a ¹⁄₁₆" gap between the stripes on the sail.*

4. Once you have all of the pieces in place, stand back and study your quilt top. Make any necessary adjustments. Following the manufacturer's directions for your fusible web, press all of the pieces to adhere them to the foundation. Allow the quilt top to cool.

FINISHING

Refer to "Quilting and Finishing" starting on page 9 to complete your quilt or "Banners" on page 12 to turn your quilt top into a banner.

Join to upper-right quadrant of pattern on page 21.

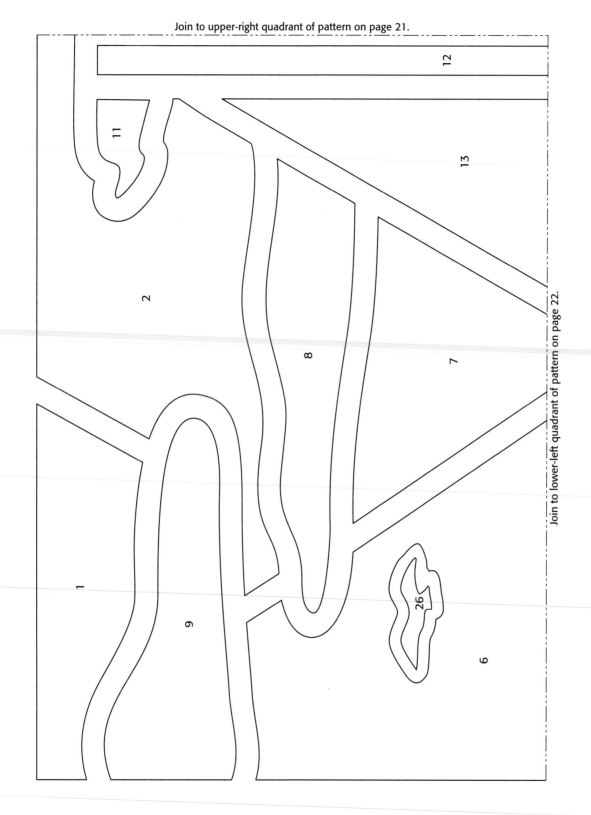

Join to lower-left quadrant of pattern on page 22.

Sailing
Upper-Left Quadrant

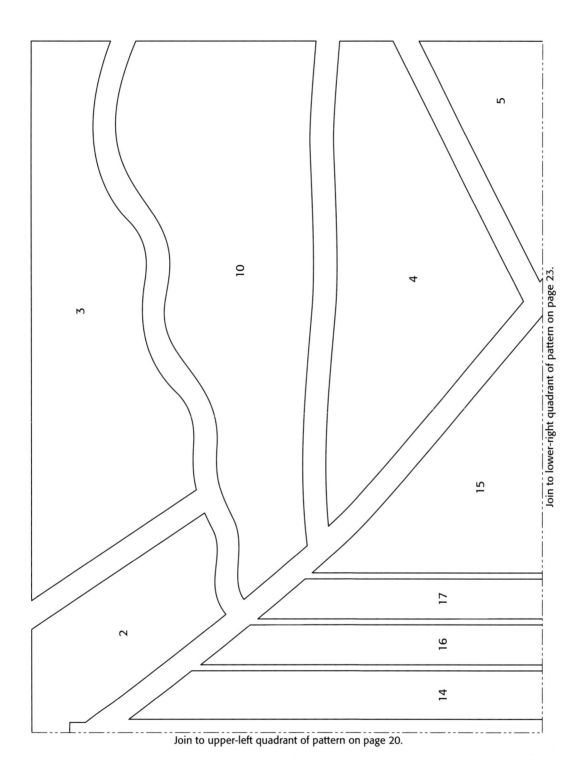

Join to lower-right quadrant of pattern on page 23.

Join to upper-left quadrant of pattern on page 20.

Sailing
Upper-Right Quadrant

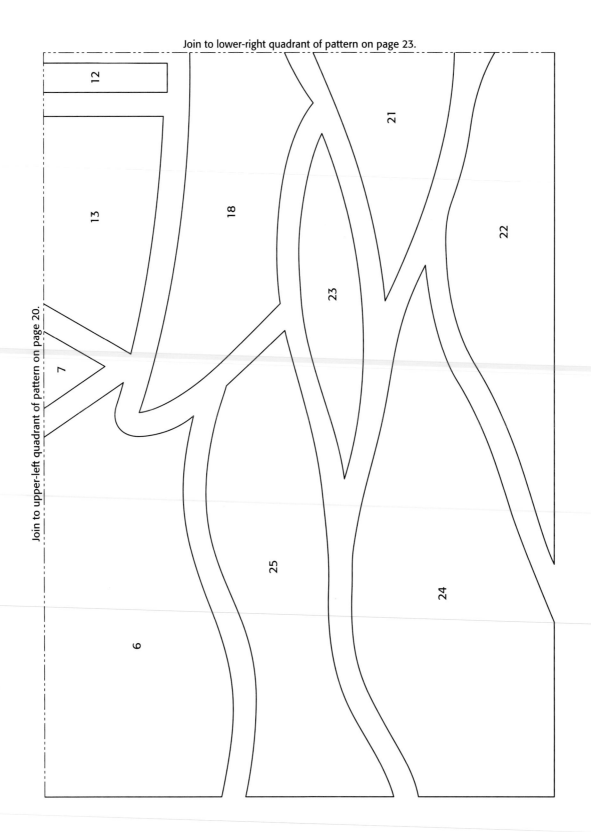

Join to lower-right quadrant of pattern on page 23.

Join to upper-left quadrant of pattern on page 20.

12

13

18

21

22

23

7

25

24

6

Sailing
Lower-Left Quadrant

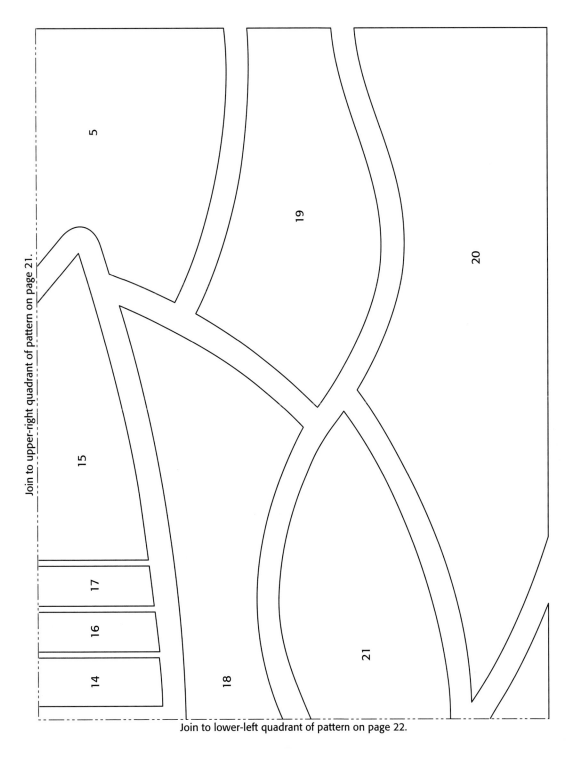

Join to upper-right quadrant of pattern on page 21.

Join to lower-left quadrant of pattern on page 22.

Sailing
Lower-Right Quadrant

Country Bouquet

Country Bouquet by Amy Whalen Helmkamp,
1999, Lake Oswego, Oregon, 13 1/2" x 18 1/2".

*Country—the very word elicits thoughts of simple pleasures,
rolling hills, open fields, dirt roads, and gardens filled to the
brim with flowers of all types in a rainbow of colors. Cut and
placed in simple containers, these flowers can also grace the
home, where they bring with them the beauty and
fragrance of the outdoors.*

MATERIALS

*All fabrics are 42" wide and 100
percent cotton unless otherwise stated.*

- ⅞ yd. black solid fabric for
  foundation, backing, binding,
  and hanging sleeve
- ⅛ yd. mottled dark green fabric
  for border strips
- 5" x 9" rectangle of mottled
  yellow-green fabric for corner
  triangle pieces 1–4
- 14" square of mottled light
  gray fabric for background
  pieces 5–15
- 7" square of mottled dark
  gray fabric for watering can
  pieces 16–18
- 6" square of mottled green
  fabric for stem and leaf
  pieces 19–27
- 7" square of mottled medium
  purple fabric for flower pieces
  28a–e, 29a–e, and 30a–e
- 1" x 3" rectangle of bright gold
  print for flower center pieces
  28f, 29f, and 30f
- ⅞ yd. fusible web
- 16½" x 21½" piece of batting
- Black cotton thread for no-sew
  fusible web, plus monofilament
  thread if you use lightweight
  fusible web

CUTTING

From the black solid fabric:

1. Cut 2 strips, each 2½" x 42", for
   the binding. Set them aside.

2. Cut a 4½" x 13" rectangle for
   the hanging sleeve. Set it aside.

3. Cut 2 pieces, each 16½" x 21½", for the foundation and the quilt backing. Set them aside.

PREPARING THE APPLIQUÉS

NOTE: *The pattern is the mirror image of your finished quilt. Should you wish to have the finished design face the same direction as the pattern, turn the pattern over and trace the pieces from the backside of the pattern.*

1. Draw the border pieces onto the fusible web. Using a ruler, draw two 1" x 12½" strips and two 1" x 15" strips. The 1" x 15" strips will be the side borders, and the 1" x 12½" strips will be the top and bottom borders.

2. Referring to "Tracing the Design onto Fusible Web" on page 7, trace the pattern pieces on pages 26–29 onto the fusible web. Group pieces together that will be cut from the same fabric. For instance, all of the background pieces (5–15) are cut from the background fabric, so trace them close together on one section of your fusible web. Likewise, group all of the flower pieces (28a–30e) together, and so on. Write the corresponding pattern number on each piece.

3. After you trace all of the pieces, cut the groups apart and fuse them to the wrong side of the appliqué fabrics. Be sure to refer to the manufacturer's instructions for using the fusible web. Cut out each shape and set the appliqués aside.

NOTE: *If you prefer not to cut out piece 18 for the cap of the watering can spout, simply trace and cut the spout as one whole piece; then color in the leading space on the quilt top with a permanent marker or embroider it with black thread.*

ASSEMBLING THE QUILT TOP

1. Using a ruler and a marking pencil, measure 2" in from each edge of the foundation fabric and draw a line the full length of each side to use as guidelines. Or see page 8 if you prefer to trace your entire pattern onto the foundation fabric.

2. Referring to the appliqué guide below and the pattern, place the appliqué pieces onto the foundation fabric. Begin with the border strips. Place the top and bottom border strips on first, laying the outside edge of each strip on the drawn line.

Appliqué Guide

Next, place the side border strips with their outside edges on the drawn lines. Leave a ¼" gap between the ends of these strips and the edges of the top and bottom strips. Use a ruler to check your spacing if desired.

3. Continuing to work from the outside edges toward the quilt center, place the remaining appliqué pieces onto the foundation fabric. Leave a ¼" gap between all of the pieces.

NOTE: *The flower centers and the end of the watering spout are exceptions to this rule. Leave an ⅛" space around the flower centers and a 1/16" space between the end of the watering spout and its cap.*

4. Once you have all of the pieces in place, stand back and study your quilt top. Make any necessary adjustments. Following the manufacturer's directions for your fusible web, press all of the pieces to adhere them to the foundation. Allow your quilt top to cool.

FINISHING

Refer to "Quilting and Finishing" starting on page 9 to complete your quilt or "Banners" on page 12 to turn your top into a banner.

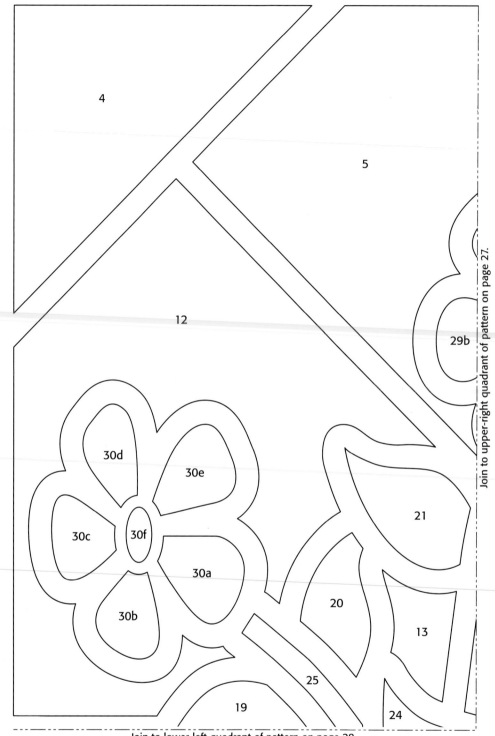

4

5

Join to upper-right quadrant of pattern on page 27.

29b

12

30d

30e

30c

30f

30a

21

30b

20

13

25

19

24

Join to lower-left quadrant of pattern on page 28.

Country Bouquet
Upper-Left Quadrant

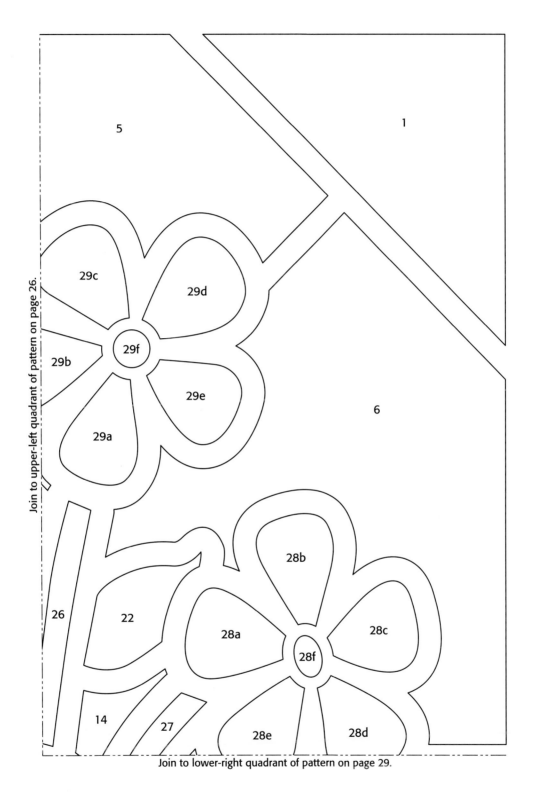

5

1

Join to upper-left quadrant of pattern on page 26.

29c

29d

29f

29b

29e

29a

6

28b

26

22

28a

28c

28f

14

27

28e

28d

Join to lower-right quadrant of pattern on page 29.

Country Bouquet
Upper-Right Quadrant

Join to upper-left quadrant of pattern on page 26.

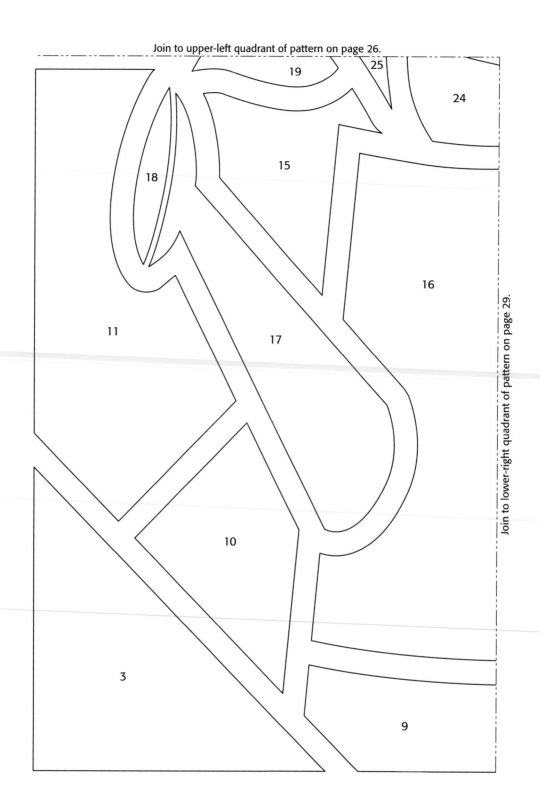

Join to lower-right quadrant of pattern on page 29.

Country Bouquet
Lower-Left Quadrant

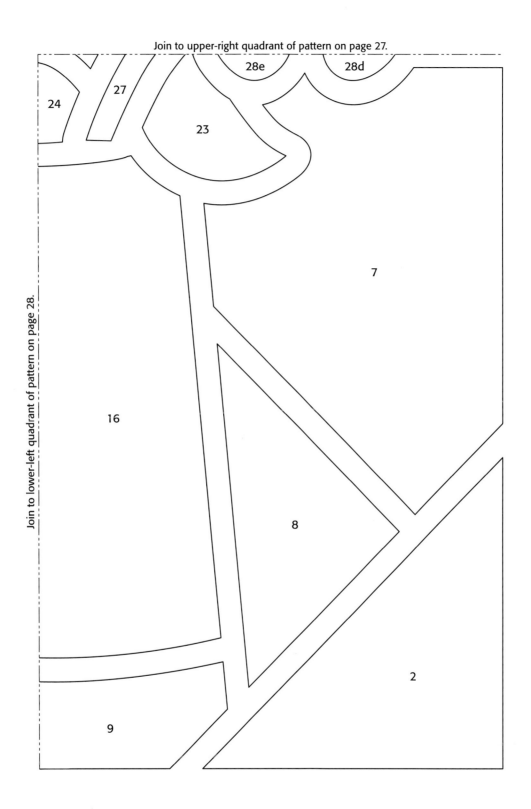

Join to upper-right quadrant of pattern on page 27.

Join to lower-left quadrant of pattern on page 28.

28e

28d

27

24

23

7

16

8

2

9

Country Bouquet
Lower-Right Quadrant

Nature's Beauty

Nature's Beauty by Amy Whalen
Helmkamp, 1999, Lake Oswego, Oregon,
14" x 16".

I have always loved to watch butterflies, with their brightly colored wings that allow them to float through the air so effortlessly. They are truly one of nature's beauties.

MATERIALS

All fabrics are 42" wide and 100 percent cotton unless otherwise stated.

- ⅔ yd. black solid fabric for foundation, backing, binding, and hanging sleeve
- ⅛ yd. or 5" x 15" rectangle of turquoise print for border strips
- 12" square of mottled light gray fabric for sky pieces 1–5
- 6" x 7" rectangle of bright yellow print for wing pieces 6–13
- 7" x 8" rectangle of mottled turquoise fabric for wing pieces 14–21
- 1½" x 5½" strip of mottled dark green fabric for butterfly body piece 22
- 7" x 9" rectangle of mottled red fabric for flower petal pieces 23–32
- 1½" x 2½" scrap of orange print for flower center piece 33
- ⅔ yd. fusible web
- 17" x 19" piece of batting
- Black cotton thread for no-sew fusible web, plus monofilament thread if you use lightweight fusible web

CUTTING

From the black solid fabric:

1. Cut 2 strips, each 2½" x 42", for the binding. Set them aside.

2. Cut a 4½" x 13½" rectangle for the hanging sleeve. Set it aside.

3. Cut 2 pieces, each 17" x 19", for the foundation and quilt backing. Set them aside.

PREPARING THE APPLIQUÉS

NOTE: *The pattern is the mirror image of your finished quilt. Should you wish to have the finished design face the same direction as the pattern, turn the pattern over and trace the pieces from the backside of the pattern.*

1. Draw the border pieces onto the fusible web. Using a ruler, draw four ¾" x 13" strips for the top, bottom, and side borders.

2. Referring to "Tracing the Design onto Fusible Web" on page 7, trace the pattern pieces on pages 32–35 onto the fusible web. Group pieces together that will be cut from the same fabric. For instance, all of the sky pieces (1–5) are cut from the mottled light gray fabric, so trace them close together on one section of your fusible web. Likewise, group the flower pieces (23–32) together, and so on. Write the corresponding pattern number on each piece.

3. After you trace all of the pieces, cut the groups apart and fuse them to the wrong side of the appliqué fabrics. Be sure to refer to the manufacturer's instructions for using the fusible web. Cut out each shape and set the appliqués aside.

ASSEMBLING THE QUILT TOP

1. Using a ruler and a marking pencil, measure 2" in from each edge of the foundation fabric and draw a line the full length of each side to use as guidelines. Or see page 8 if you prefer to trace your entire pattern onto the foundation fabric.

2. Referring to the appliqué guide below and the pattern, place the appliqué pieces onto the foundation fabric. Begin with the border strips. Place the top and bottom border strips on first, laying the outside edge of each strip on the drawn line. Next, place the side border strips with their outside edges on the drawn lines. Leave a ¼" gap between the ends of these strips and the edges of the top and bottom strips. Use a ruler to check your spacing if desired.

Appliqué Guide

3. Continuing to work from the outside edges toward the quilt center, place the remaining appliqué pieces onto the foundation fabric. Leave a ¼" gap between all of the pieces.

Note: *The butterfly's wings are the exception to this rule. There is only a ¹⁄₁₆" gap between the wing tips and main part of the wing. There is a ⅛" gap between the upper and lower wings and between the wings and butterfly's body.*

4. Once you have all of the pieces in place, stand back and study your quilt top. Make any necessary adjustments. Following the manufacturer's directions for your fusible web, press all of the pieces to adhere them to the foundation. Allow the quilt top to cool.

FINISHING

Refer to "Quilting and Finishing" starting on page 9 to complete your quilt or "Banners" on page 12 to turn your top into a banner.

1

6

14

5

7

15

8

16

Join to upper-right quadrant of pattern on page 33.

Join to lower-left quadrant of pattern on page 34.

Nature's Beauty
Upper-Left Quadrant

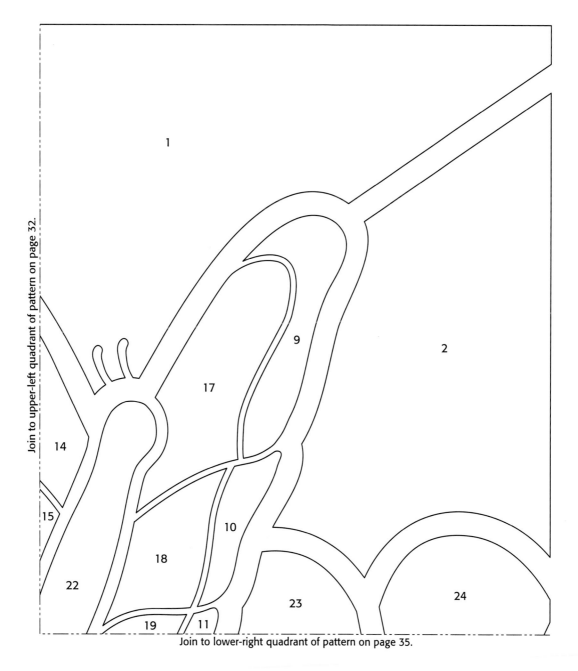

Join to upper-left quadrant of pattern on page 32.

Join to lower-right quadrant of pattern on page 35.

Nature's Beauty
Upper-Right Quadrant

Join to upper-left quadrant of pattern on page 32.

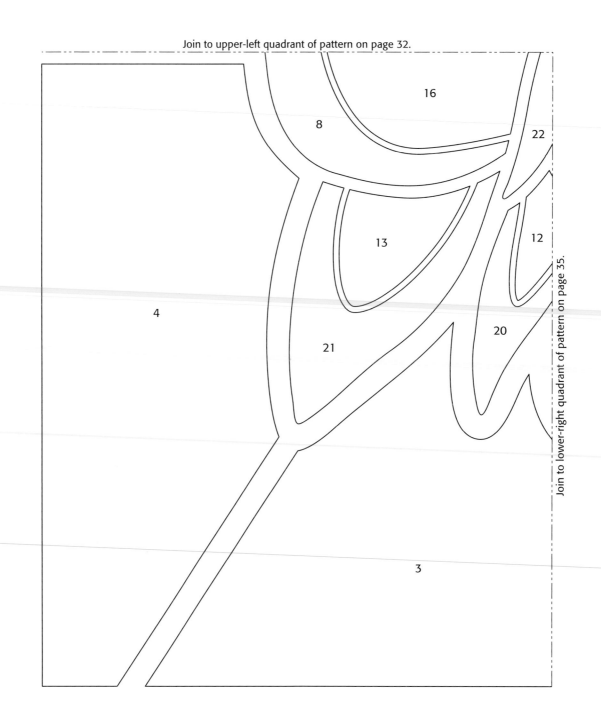

Join to lower-right quadrant of pattern on page 35.

Nature's Beauty
Lower-Left Quadrant

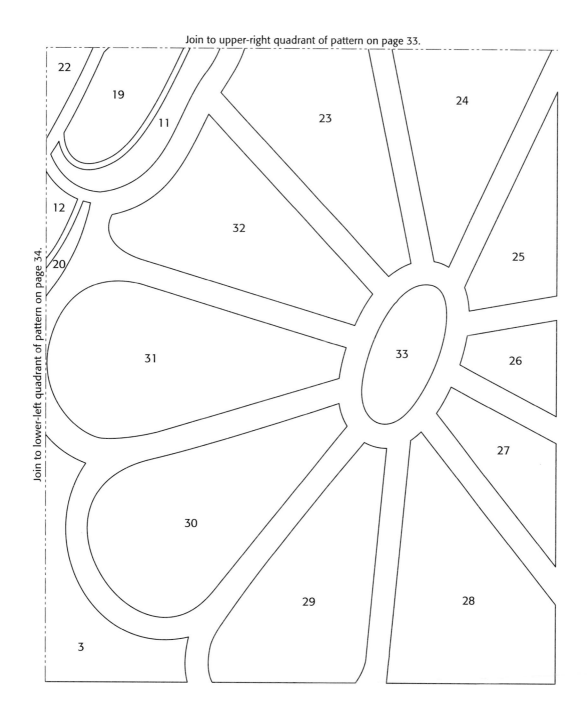

Join to upper-right quadrant of pattern on page 33.

22

19

11

12

20

3

Join to lower-left quadrant of pattern on page 34.

32

31

30

23

24

25

33

26

27

29

28

Nature's Beauty
Lower-Right Quadrant

Rose in Bloom

Rose in Bloom by Amy Whalen Helmkamp, 1999, Lake Oswego, Oregon, 10½" x 33".

Roses are a favorite flower of many, and it's easy to understand why, with their sweet fragrance and elegant beauty. This design is pretty hanging by an entryway, but it can also be used as a table runner.

MATERIALS

All fabrics are 42" wide and 100 percent cotton unless otherwise stated.

- 1⅛ yd. black solid fabric for foundation, backing, binding, and hanging sleeve
- 10" square of mottled dark turquoise fabric for border strips
- 11" x 24" rectangle of mottled light blue fabric for background pieces 1–15
- 3" x 8" rectangle of red solid fabric for rose pieces 16a–18h
- 4" x 9" rectangle of mottled medium green fabric for stem and leaf pieces 19–27
- 1 yd. fusible web
- 13½" x 36" piece of batting
- Black cotton thread for no-sew fusible web, plus monofilament thread if you use lightweight fusible web

CUTTING

From the black solid fabric:

1. Cut 3 strips, each 2½" x 42", for the binding. Set them aside.

2. Cut a 4½" x 10" strip for the hanging sleeve. Set it aside.

3. Cut 2 pieces, each 13½" x 36", for the foundation and the quilt backing. Set them aside.

PREPARING THE APPLIQUÉS

NOTE: *The pattern is the mirror image of your finished quilt. Should you wish to have the finished design face the same direction as the pattern, turn the pattern over and trace the pieces from the backside of the pattern.*

1. Draw the border pieces onto the fusible web. Using a ruler, draw six 1" x 9" strips, two 1" x 9½" strips, and two ¾" x 9½" strips. The 1" x 9" strips will be the side borders, the 1" x 9½" strips will be the top and bottom borders, and the ¾" x 9½" strips will be used to separate the individual rose panels.

2. Referring to "Tracing the Design onto Fusible Web" on page 7, trace the pattern pieces on pages 39–41 onto the fusible web. Group pieces together that will be cut from the same fabric. For instance, all of the background pieces (1–15) are cut from the mottled light blue fabric, so trace them close together on one section of your fusible web. Likewise, group all of the rose pieces (16a–18h) together, and so on. Write the corresponding pattern number on each piece.

3. After you trace all of the pieces, cut the groups apart and fuse them to the wrong side of the appliqué fabrics you have chosen. Be sure to refer to the manufacturer's instructions for using the fusible web. Cut out each shape, and set the appliqués aside.

ASSEMBLING THE QUILT TOP

1. Using a ruler and a marking pencil, measure 2" in from each edge of the foundation fabric, and draw a line the full length of each side to use as guidelines. Or see page 8 if you prefer to trace your entire pattern onto the foundation fabric.

2. Referring to the appliqué guide below right and the pattern, place the appliqué pieces onto the foundation fabric. Begin with the border strips. Place the top and bottom border strips on first, laying the outside edge of each strip on the drawn line. Next, place the side border strips, which consist of 3 segments, with their outside edges on the drawn lines. Leave a ¼" gap between the ends of the top and bottom side border segments and the edges of the top and bottom border strips. Leave a 1¼" gap between the top and middle side border segments, as well as between the bottom and middle side border segments. You'll need these 1¼" spaces so that you can place the ¾" x 9½" strips between the rose panels. Use a ruler to check your spacing if you desire.

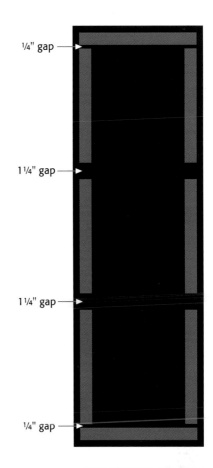

¼" gap

1¼" gap

1¼" gap

¼" gap

Appliqué Guide

3. Continuing to work from the outside edges toward the quilt center, place the remaining appliqué pieces onto the foundation fabric. Leave a ¼" gap between all of the pieces.

   NOTE: *The rose pieces are the exception to this rule. There is only a ⅛" gap between the rose petals, the stem and the petals, and the leaves and the stem.*

4. Once you have all of the pieces in place, stand back and study your quilt top. Make any necessary adjustments. Following the manufacturer's directions for your fusible web, press all of the pieces to adhere them to the foundation. Allow the quilt top to cool.

FINISHING

Refer to "Quilting and Finishing" starting on page 9 to complete your quilt or "Banners" on page 12 to turn your quilt top into a banner.

1

2

16

16a

16b

20

5

19

21

4

3

Rose in Bloom
Top Motif

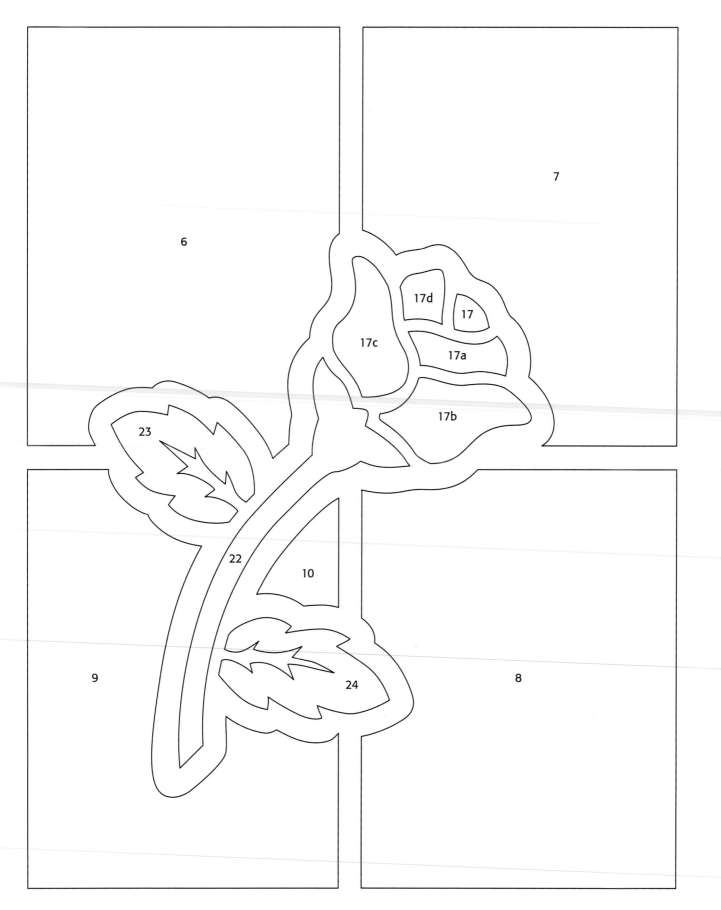

6

7

17d

17

17c

17a

17b

23

22

10

9

24

8

Rose in Bloom
Middle Motif

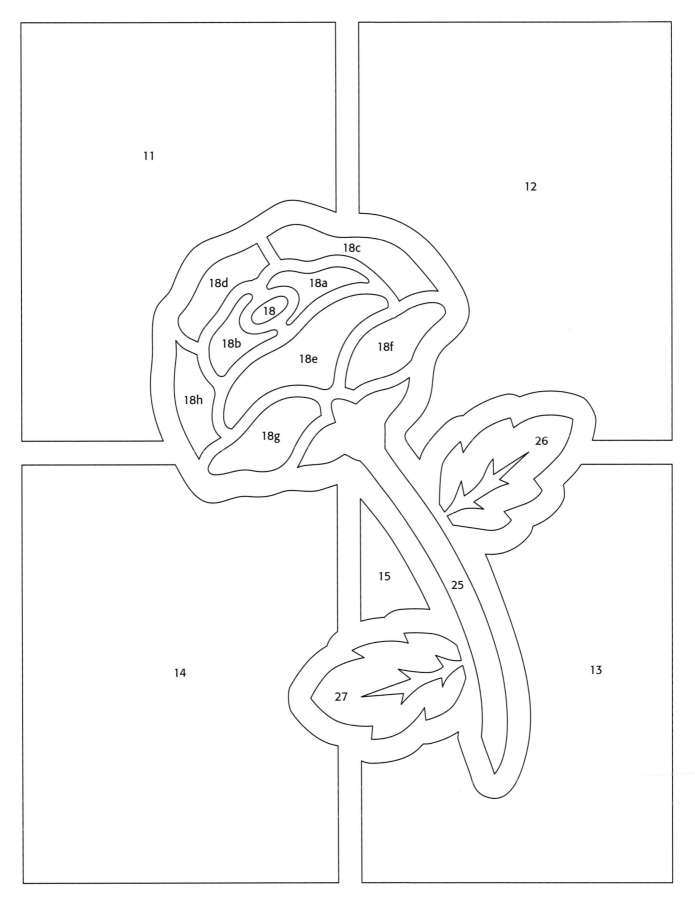

Rose in Bloom
Bottom Motif

Home Tweet Home

Home Tweet Home by Amy Whalen
Helmkamp, 1999, Lake Oswego, Oregon,
14" x 18".

This pretty bluebird—one of my favorite harbingers of spring—reminds us that it's always nice to come home to roost.

MATERIALS

All fabrics are 42" wide and 100 percent cotton unless otherwise stated.

- ⅞ yd. black solid fabric for foundation, backing, binding, and hanging sleeve
- ⅛ yd. or 4" x 17" rectangle of mottled dark blue fabric for border strips
- 14" square of mottled light blue fabric for sky pieces 1–12
- 5" x 8" rectangle of white print for cloud pieces 13–15
- 5" square of mottled bright blue fabric for bird pieces 16–18
- 1" square of gold print for beak piece 19
- 2" x 4" rectangle of mottled dark brown fabric for birdhouse roof piece 20
- 5" square of mottled medium rust fabric for birdhouse pieces 21–23
- 1" x 6" rectangle of mottled light brown fabric for birdhouse post pieces 24–25
- 4" x 12" rectangle of mottled orange fabric for flower pieces 26–28
- 1" x 3" rectangle dark gold print for flower center pieces 26a, 27a, and 28a
- 4" x 5" rectangle of mottled green fabric for stem and leaf pieces 29–33
- ⅞ yd. fusible web
- 17" x 21" piece of batting
- Black cotton thread for no-sew fusible web, plus monofilament thread if you use lightweight fusible web

CUTTING

From the black solid fabric:

1. Cut 2 strips, each 2½" x 42", for the binding. Set them aside.

2. Cut a 4½" x 13½" rectangle for the hanging sleeve. Set it aside.

3. Cut 2 pieces, each 17" x 21", for the foundation and the quilt backing. Set them aside.

PREPARING THE APPLIQUÉS

NOTE: *The pattern is the mirror image of your finished quilt. Should you wish to have the finished design face the same direction as the pattern, turn the pattern over and trace the pieces from the backside of the pattern.*

1. Draw the border pieces onto the fusible web. Using a ruler, draw two ¾" x 15" strips and two ¾" x 13" strips. The ¾" x 15" strips will be the side borders, and the ¾" x 13" strips will be the top and bottom borders.

2. Referring to "Tracing the Design onto Fusible Web" on page 7, trace the pattern pieces on pages 44–47 onto the fusible web. Group pieces together that will be cut from the same fabric. For instance, all of the sky pieces (1–12) are cut from the mottled light blue fabric, so trace them close to-gether on one section of your fusible web. Likewise, group the cloud pieces (13–15) to-gether, and so on. Write the corresponding pattern number on each piece.

3. After you trace all of the pieces, cut the groups apart and fuse them to the wrong side of the appliqué fabrics. Be sure to refer to the manufacturer's instructions for using the fusible web. Cut out each shape, and set the appliqués aside.

NOTE: *When you cut out the bird, cut out the hole for the bird's eye. Also cut out the hole in the bird-house. If you prefer, you may color in the eye with a permanent mark-er or embroider it with black thread.*

ASSEMBLING THE QUILT TOP

1. Using a ruler and a marking pencil, measure 2" in from each edge of the foundation fabric, and draw a line the full length of each side to use as guide-lines. Or see page 8 if you pre-fer to trace your entire pattern onto the foundation fabric.

2. Referring to the appliqué guide at right and the pattern, place the appliqué pieces onto the foundation fabric. Begin with the border strips. Place the top and bottom border strips on first, laying the outside edge of each strip on the drawn line. Next, place the side border strips with their outside edges on the drawn lines. Leave a ¼" gap between the ends of these strips and the edges of the top and bottom strips. Use a ruler to check your spacing if you desire.

Appliqué Guide

3. Continuing to work from the outside edges toward the quilt center, place the remaining pieces onto the foundation fab-ric. Leave a ¼" gap between all of the pieces.

NOTE: *The bird's wings, birdhouse front, and flower centers are excep-tions to this rule. Leave only a ¹⁄₁₆" gap between the centers of the flower and the petals, and between the bird's beak and body. There is a ⅛" gap between the bird's wings and its body, and between the birdhouse's front and the peak of the roof.*

4. Once you have all of the pieces in place, stand back and study your quilt top. Make any neces-sary adjustments. Following the manufacturer's directions for your fusible web, press all of the pieces to adhere them to the foundation. Allow your quilt top to cool.

FINISHING

Refer to "Quilting and Finishing" starting on page 9 to complete your quilt or "Banners" on page 12 to turn your quilt top into a banner.

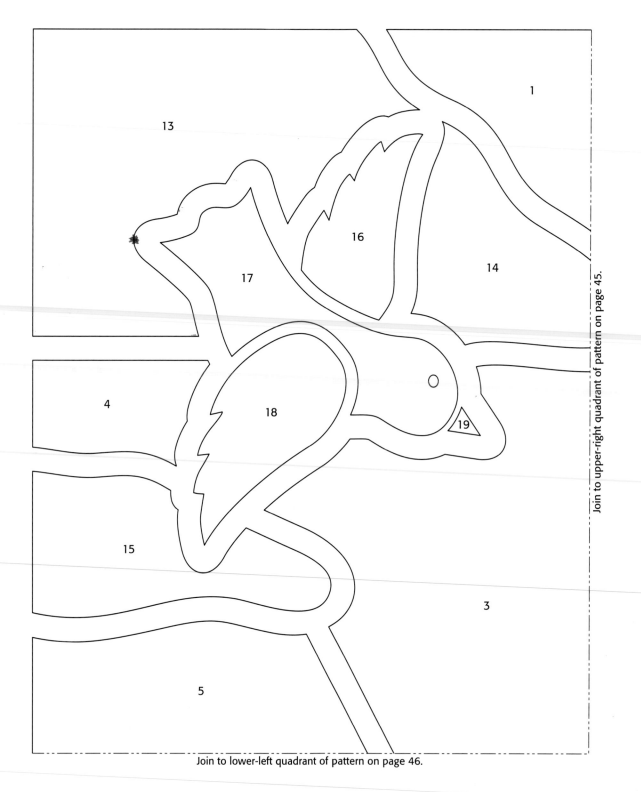

Join to upper-right quadrant of pattern on page 45.

Join to lower-left quadrant of pattern on page 46.

Home Tweet Home
Upper-Left Quadrant

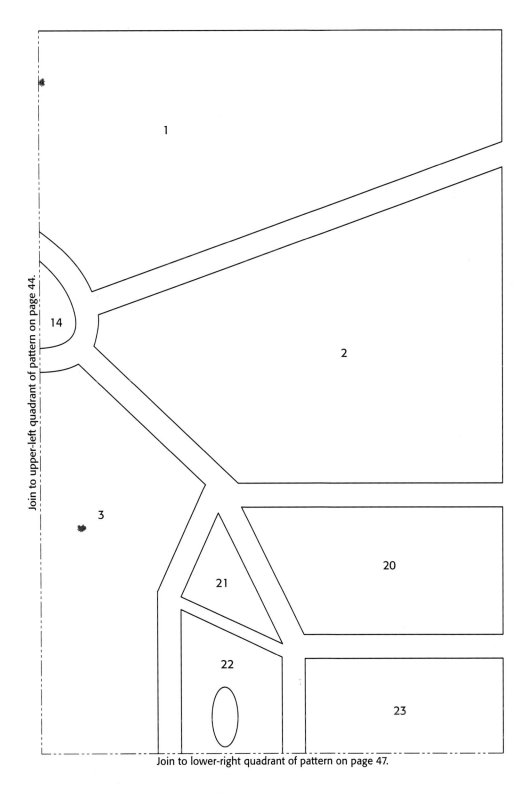

Join to upper-left quadrant of pattern on page 44.

Join to lower-right quadrant of pattern on page 47.

Home Tweet Home
Upper-Right Quadrant

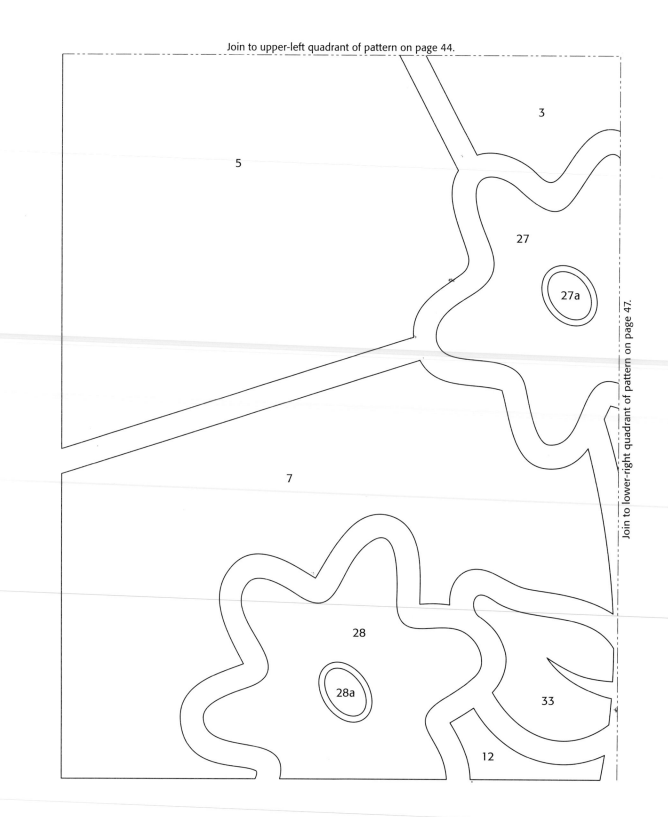

Join to upper-left quadrant of pattern on page 44.

3

5

27

27a

Join to lower-right quadrant of pattern on page 47.

7

28

28a

33

12

Home Tweet Home
Lower-Left Quadrant

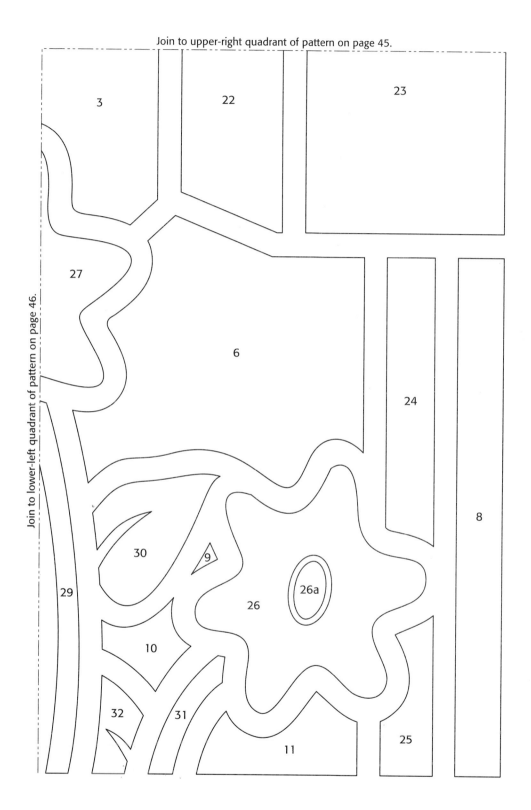

Join to upper-right quadrant of pattern on page 45.

Join to lower-left quadrant of pattern on page 46.

3

22

23

27

6

24

8

30

9

26a

29

26

10

32

31

25

11

Home Tweet Home
Lower-Right Quadrant

Tulip Cameo

Tulip Cameo by Amy Whalen Helmkamp,
1999, Lake Oswego, Oregon, 16" x 16".

I've designed three variations on this flower cameo pattern. Make one with your favorite flower, or make three to hang together as a set. The patterns for the quilts "Iris Cameo" and "Rose Cameo" use the same background pieces as "Tulip Cameo." You'll find the patterns and fabric requirements for "Iris Cameo" and "Rose Cameo" at the end of the directions for "Tulip Cameo."

MATERIALS

All fabrics are 42" wide and 100 percent cotton unless otherwise stated.

- ⅞ yd. black solid fabric for foundation, backing, binding, and hanging sleeve
- ⅛ yd. or 5" x 17" rectangle of mottled dark green fabric for border strips
- 14" square of mottled pink fabric for background pieces 1–6
- 7" x 9" rectangle of mottled light green fabric for center background pieces 7–10
- 3" square of dark pink print for tulip pieces 11–13
- 4" x 5" rectangle of mottled green fabric for stem and leaf pieces 14–16
- ¾ yd. fusible web
- 19" square of batting
- Black cotton thread for no-sew fusible web, plus monofilament thread if you use lightweight fusible web

CUTTING

From the solid black fabric:

1. Cut 2 strips, each 2½" x 42", for the binding. Set them aside.

2. Cut a 4½" x 15½" rectangle for the hanging sleeve. Set it aside.

3. Cut 2 pieces, each 19" x 19", for the foundation and the quilt backing. Set them aside.

PREPARING THE APPLIQUÉS

NOTE: *The pattern is the mirror image of your finished quilt. Should you wish to have the finished design face the same direction as the pattern, turn the pattern over and trace the pieces from the backside of the pattern.*

1. Draw the border pieces onto the fusible web. Using a ruler, draw two 1" x 15" strips and two 1" x 12½" strips. The 1" x 15" strips will be the top and bottom borders, and the 1" x 12½" strips will be the side borders.

2. Referring to "Tracing the Design onto Fusible Web" on page 7, trace the pattern pieces on pages 50–53 onto the fusible web. Group pieces together that will be cut from the same fabric. For instance, all of the background pieces (1–6) are cut from the mottled pink fabric, so trace them close together on one section of your fusible web. Likewise, group the tulip pieces (11–13) together, and so on. Write the corresponding pattern number on each piece.

3. After you trace all of the pieces, cut the groups apart and fuse them to the wrong side of the appliqué fabrics. Be sure to refer to the manufacturer's instructions for using the fusible web. Cut out each shape.

ASSEMBLING THE QUILT TOP

1. Using a ruler and a marking pencil, measure 2" in from each edge of the foundation fabric and draw a line the full length of each side to use as guidelines. Or see page 8 if you prefer to trace your entire pattern onto the foundation fabric.

2. Referring to the appliqué guide below and the pattern, place the appliqué pieces onto the foundation fabric. Begin with the border strips. Place the top and bottom border strips on first, laying the outside edge of each strip on the drawn line. Next, place the side border strips with their outside edges on the drawn lines. Leave a ¼" gap between the ends of these strips and the edges of the top and bottom strips. Use a ruler to check your spacing if you desire.

Appliqué Guide

3. Continuing to work from the outside edges toward the quilt center, place the remaining appliqué pieces onto the foundation fabric. Leave a ¼" gap between all of the pieces.

    NOTE: *The flower is the exception to this rule. Leave only a ⅛" gap between the flower petals, between the stem and petals, and between the leaves and stem.*

4. Once you have all of the pieces in place, stand back and study your quilt top. Make any necessary adjustments. Following the manufacturer's directions for your fusible web, press all of the pieces to adhere them to the foundation. Allow your quilt top to cool.

FINISHING

Refer to "Quilting and Finishing" starting on page 9 to complete your quilt or "Banners" on page 12 to turn your top into a banner.

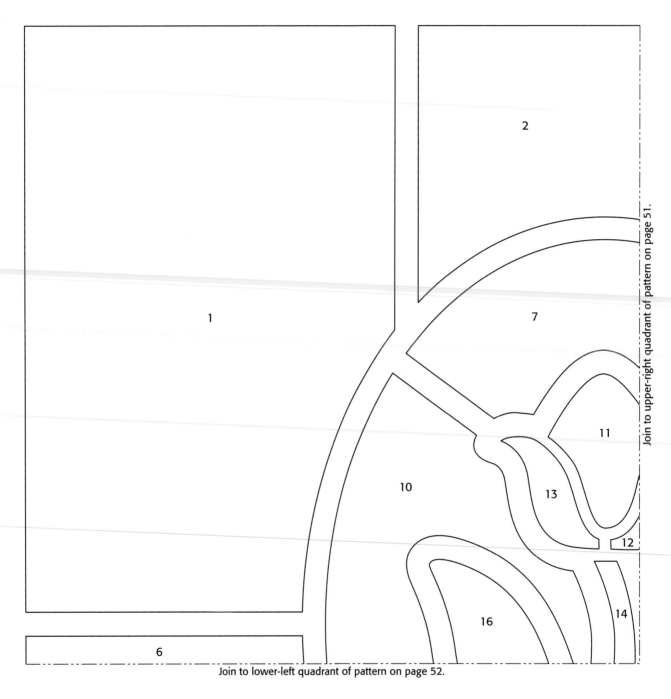

1

2

7

11

10

13

12

16

14

Join to upper-right quadrant of pattern on page 51.

6

Join to lower-left quadrant of pattern on page 52.

Tulip Cameo
Upper-Left Quadrant

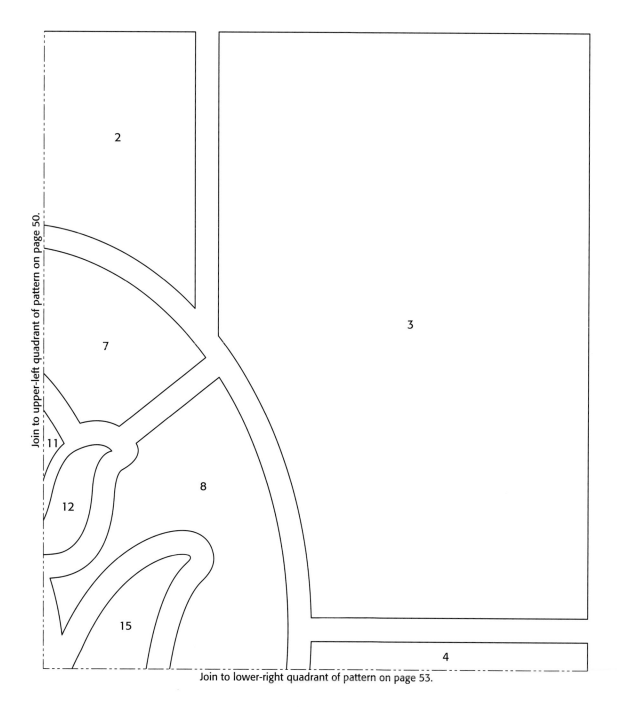

Join to upper-left quadrant of pattern on page 50.

Join to lower-right quadrant of pattern on page 53.

Tulip Cameo
Upper-Right Quadrant

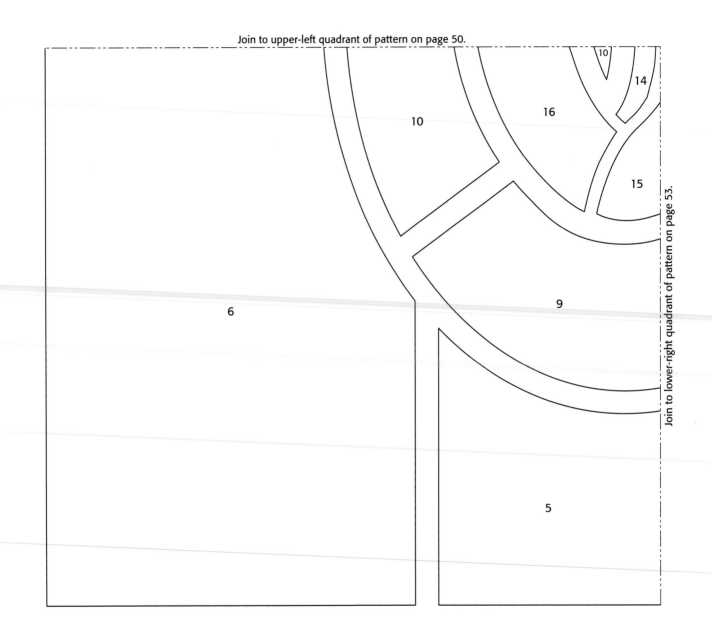

Join to upper-left quadrant of pattern on page 50.

10

10

14

16

15

6

9

Join to lower-right quadrant of pattern on page 53.

5

Tulip Cameo
Lower-Left Quadrant

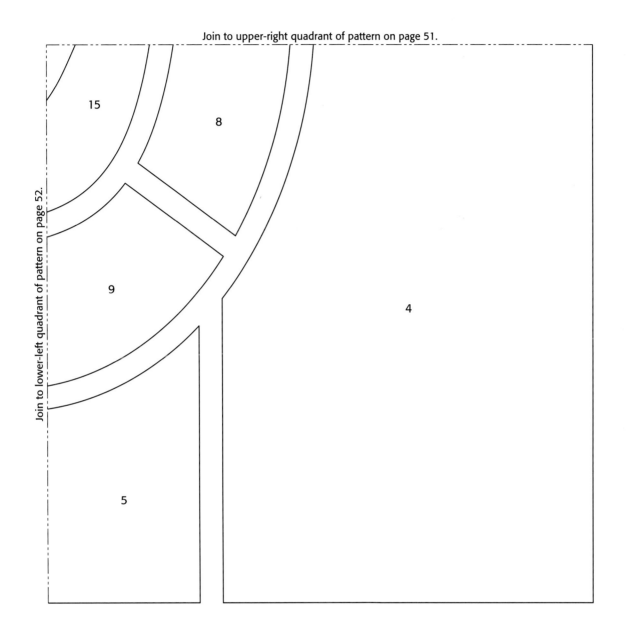

Join to upper-right quadrant of pattern on page 51.

Join to lower-left quadrant of pattern on page 52.

15

8

9

4

5

Tulip Cameo
Lower-Right Quadrant

Rose Cameo

MATERIALS

Use the same materials list as for "Tulip Cameo" on page 48, but omit the fabrics for pieces 7–16 for the tulip and tulip background. Replace those fabrics with the following:

- ◆ 7" x 9" piece of mottled light green fabric for rose background pieces 7–10
- ◆ 2" square of red solid for the rose pieces 11–13
- ◆ 4" square of mottled green fabric for stem and leaf pieces 14–17

ASSEMBLING THE QUILT

Refer to the directions for "Tulip Cameo" on page 49 to construct this quilt.

Rose Cameo by Amy Whalen Helmkamp, 1999, Lake Oswego, Oregon, 16" x 16".

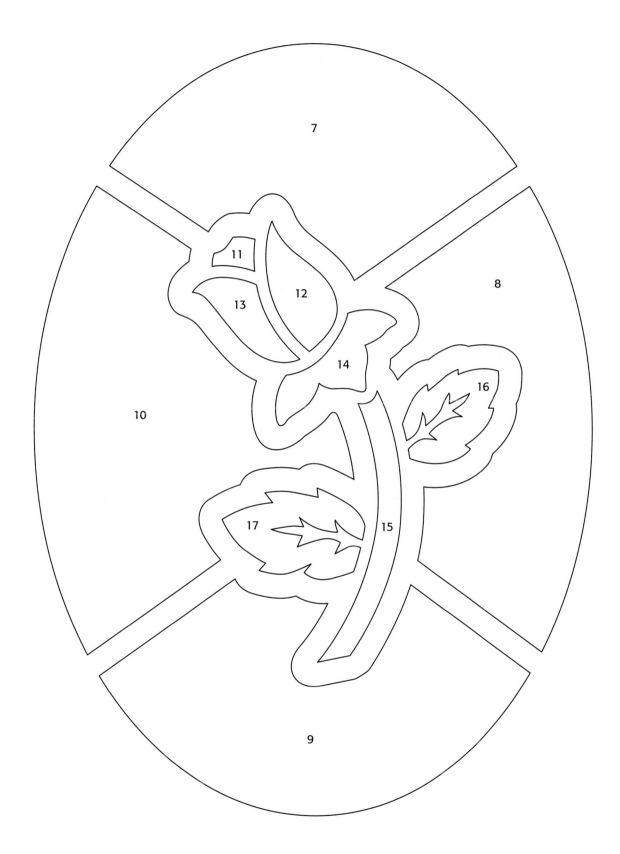

Rose Cameo

Iris Cameo

MATERIALS

Use the same materials list as for "Tulip Cameo" on page 48, but omit pieces 7–16 for the tulip and tulip background. Replace those fabrics with the following:

♦ 7" x 9" piece of light green mottled fabric for iris background pieces 7–12
♦ 4" square of purple mottled fabric for iris pieces 13–16
♦ 1" square of bright gold print for iris center piece 17
♦ 4" x 5" piece mottled green fabric for stem and leaf pieces 18–20

ASSEMBLING THE QUILT

Refer to the directions for "Tulip Cameo" on page 49 to construct this quilt.

Iris Cameo by Amy Whalen Helmkamp,
1999, Lake Oswego, Oregon, 16" x 16".

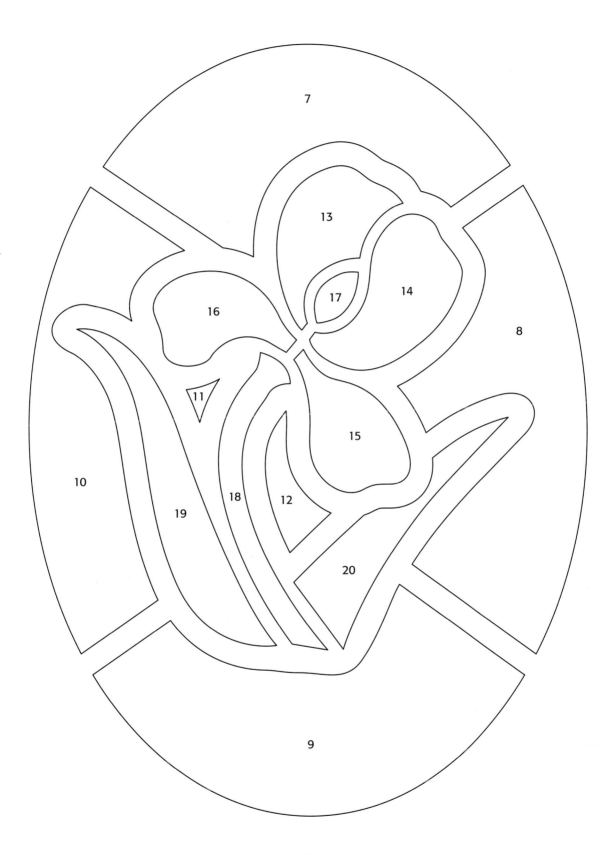

Iris Cameo

Aquarium

Aquarium by Amy Whalen Helmkamp,
1999, Lake Oswego, Oregon, 26" x 20".

Brightly colored tropical fish swimming through crystal clear blue water is a sight that brings tranquillity to the beholder. Hang this quilt in your office, family room, or other spot where you spend a lot of time so you can enjoy its serene effect.

MATERIALS

All fabrics are 42" wide and 100 percent cotton unless otherwise stated.

- 1⅝ yd. black solid fabric for foundation, backing, binding, and hanging sleeve
- ¼ yd. blue-and-green print for border strips
- 18" x 24" rectangle of aqua print for water pieces 1–15
- Scraps of several brightly colored fabrics in different colors (refer to the color photo for ideas) for the fish pieces 16a–21f
- 7" x 9" rectangle of mottled light green fabric for sea grass pieces 22–25
- 6" x 8" rectangle of mottled green fabric for seaweed piece 26
- 3" x 6" rectangle of mottled gray fabric for seashell pieces 27–32
- 2½" x 3½" rectangle of tan print for snail shell piece 33
- 1" x 2" rectangle of mottled brown fabric for snail head piece 34
- 1⅔ yd. fusible web
- 23" x 29" piece of batting
- Black cotton thread for no-sew fusible web, plus monofilament thread if you use lightweight fusible web

CUTTING

From the black solid fabric:

1. Cut 3 strips, each 2½" x 42", for the binding. Set them aside.

2. Cut a 4½" x 25½" rectangle for the hanging sleeve. Set it aside.

3. Cut 2 pieces, each 23" x 29", for the foundation and quilt backing. Set them aside.

PREPARING THE APPLIQUÉS

NOTE: *The pattern is the mirror image of your finished quilt. Should you wish to have the finished design face the same direction as the pattern, turn the pattern over and trace the pieces from the backside of the pattern.*

1. Draw the border pieces onto the fusible web. Using a ruler, draw two 1¼" x 25" strips and two 1¼" x 16" strips. The 1¼" x 25" strips will be the top and bottom borders, and the 1¼" x 16" strips will be the side borders.

2. Referring to "Tracing the Design onto Fusible Web" on page 7, trace the pattern pieces on pages 60–65 onto the fusible web. Group pieces together that will be cut from the same fabric. For instance, all of the water pieces (1–15) are cut from the same aqua print, so trace them close together on one section of your fusible web. Likewise, group the seashell pieces (27–32) together, and so on. Decide what colors you will be using for the fish, and group all of the parts that will be the same color together. Write the corresponding pattern number on each piece.

As an alternative, you may choose to make the fish body one solid piece. To do this, simply trace around the outside of the body, eliminating the individual pieces but still leaving the fins and tail as separate pieces.

3. After you trace all of the pieces, cut the groups apart and fuse them to the wrong side of the appliqué fabrics. Be sure to refer to the manufacturer's instructions for using the fusible web. Cut out each shape and set the appliqués aside. You will need to cut out the fish eyes and the holes in the seaweed. As an alternative, you may color them in with a black permanent marker or embroider them with black thread.

ASSEMBLING THE QUILT TOP

1. Using a ruler and a marking pencil, measure 2" in from each edge of the foundation fabric, and draw a line the full length of each side to use as guidelines. Or see page 8 if you prefer to trace your entire pattern onto the foundation fabric.

2. Referring to the appliqué guide at right and the pattern, begin placing the appliqué pieces onto the foundation fabric. Begin with the border strips. Place the top and bottom border strips on first, laying the outside edge of each strip on the drawn line. Next, place the side border strips with their outside edges on the drawn lines. Leave a ¼" gap between the ends of these strips and the edges of the top and bottom strips. Use a ruler to check your spacing if desired.

Appliqué Guide

3. Continuing to work from the outside edges toward the quilt center, place the remaining appliqué pieces onto the foundation fabric. Leave a ¼" gap between all of the pieces.

NOTE: *The fish body, snail, and seashell pieces are the exceptions to this rule. Leave only a 1/16" gap between these pieces.*

4. Once you have all of the pieces in place, stand back and study your quilt top. Make any necessary adjustments. Following the manufacturer's directions for your fusible web, press all of the pieces to adhere them to the foundation. Allow your quilt top to cool.

FINISHING

Refer to "Quilting and Finishing" starting on page 9 to complete your quilt or "Banners" on page 12 to turn your top into a banner.

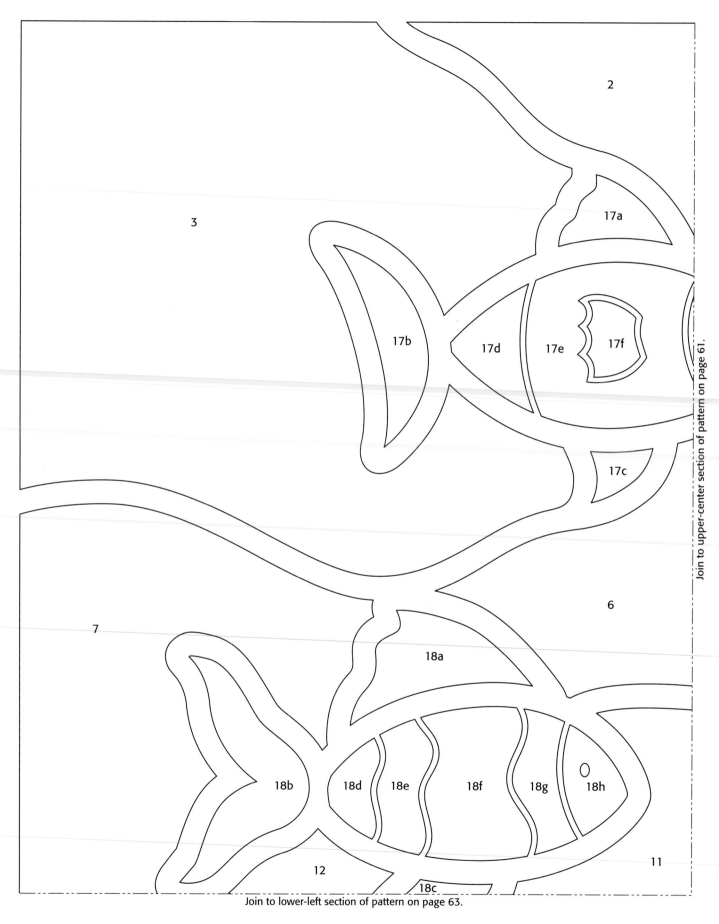

2

3

17a

17b

17d

17e

17f

17c

Join to upper-center section of pattern on page 61.

6

7

18a

18b

18d

18e

18f

18g

18h

12

11

18c

Join to lower-left section of pattern on page 63.

Aquarium
Upper-Left Section

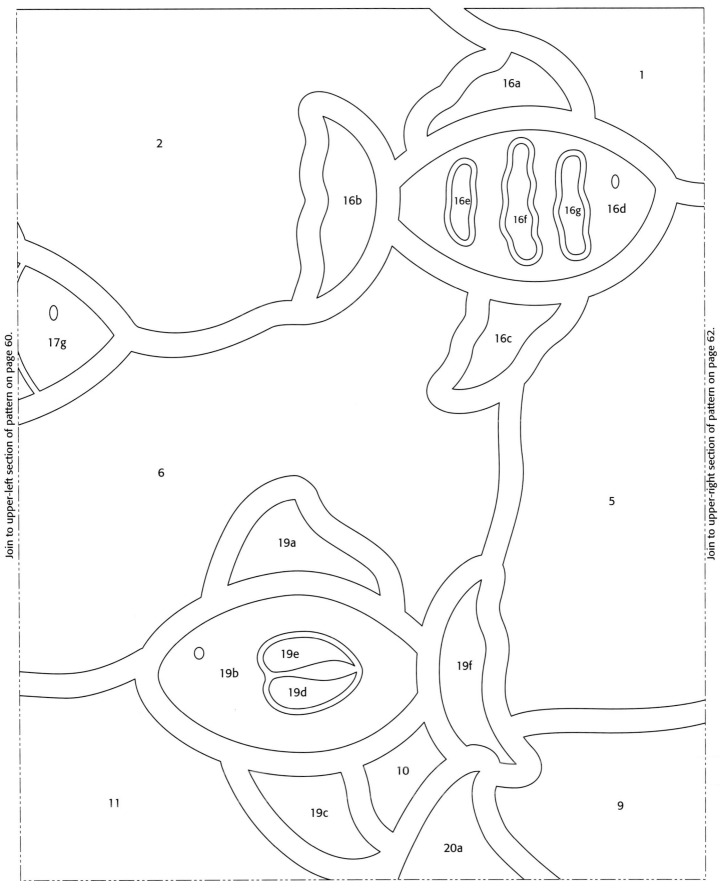

Join to upper-left section of pattern on page 60.

Join to upper-right section of pattern on page 62.

Join to lower-center section of pattern on page 64.

Aquarium
Upper-Center Section

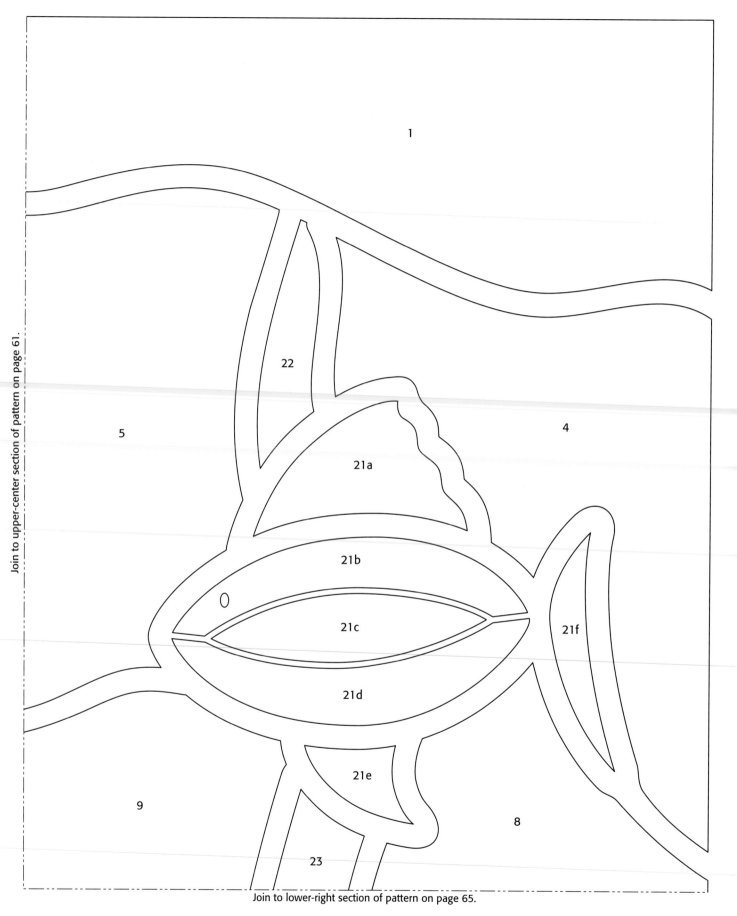

Join to upper-center section of pattern on page 61.

1

22

5

21a

4

21b

21c

21f

21d

21e

9

8

23

Join to lower-right section of pattern on page 65.

Aquarium
Upper-Right Section

Join to upper-left section of pattern on page 60.

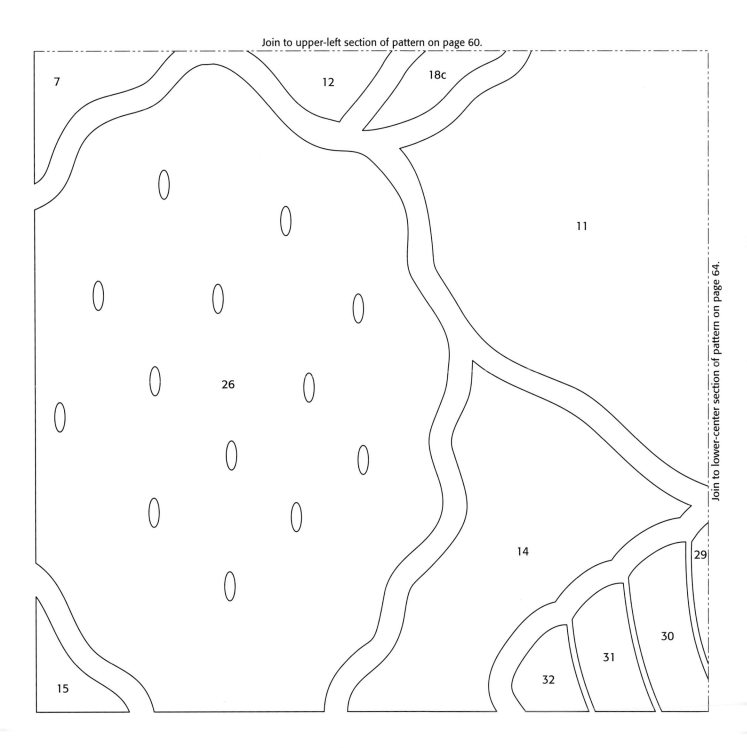

Join to lower-center section of pattern on page 64.

Aquarium
Lower-Left Section

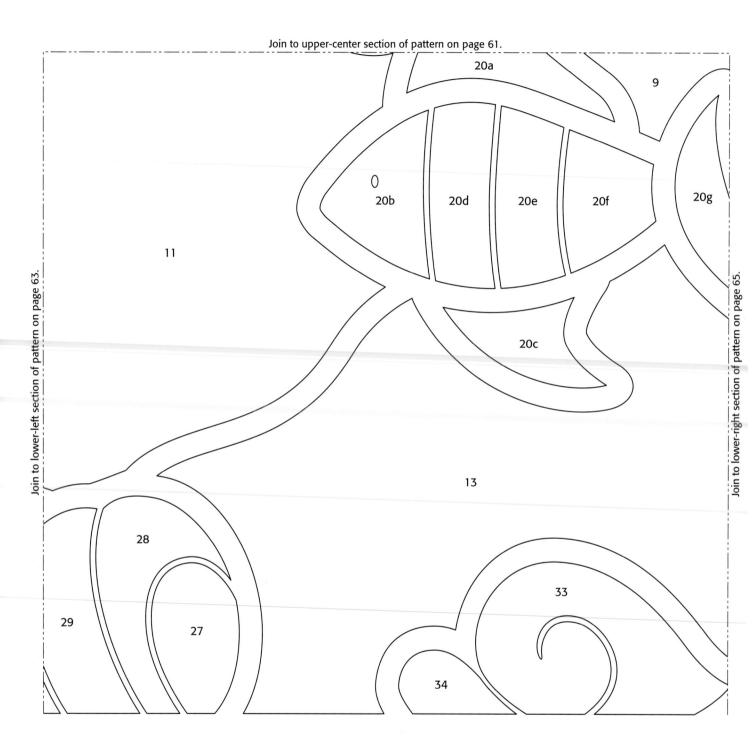

Join to upper-center section of pattern on page 61.

Join to lower-right section of pattern on page 63.

Join to lower-right section of pattern on page 65.

20a

9

20b

20d

20e

20f

20g

11

20c

13

28

33

29

27

34

Aquarium
Lower-Center Section

Join to upper-right section of pattern on page 62.

Join to lower-center section of pattern on page 64.

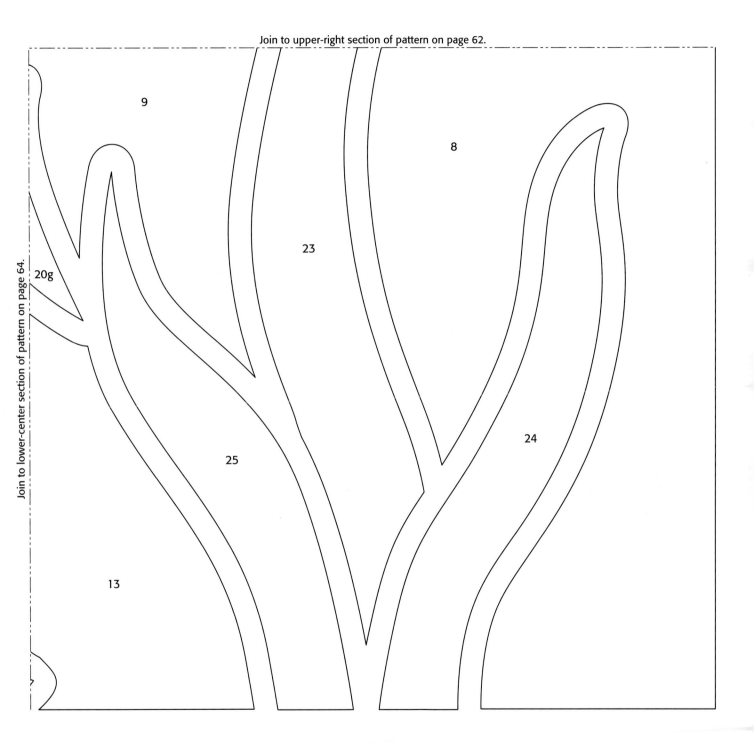

9

8

23

20g

24

25

13

Aquarium
Lower-Right Section

Teatime

Teatime by Amy Whalen Helmkamp, 1999,
Lake Oswego, Oregon, 15" x 17".

What could be more relaxing than teatime? Whether you
enjoy your favorite brew as you cozy up with a good book or
at the table chatting with a good friend, "Teatime" is sure to
invoke some pleasant memories. Choose from two border
options: one made with templates that give the look of a
picture frame, and one made with straight strips.

MATERIALS

*All fabrics are 42" wide and 100
percent cotton unless otherwise stated.*

- ⅞ yd. black solid fabric for
  foundation, backing, binding,
  and hanging sleeve
- ¼ yd. or 9" x 17" rectangle of
  blue print for either border
  option (border templates A, B,
  and C or straight strips)
- 8" x 18" rectangle of mottled
  peach fabric for background
  pieces 1–8
- 3" x 4" rectangle of mottled
  dark rust fabric for picture
  frame border pieces 9–12
- 3" x 4" rectangle of mottled
  pale yellow fabric for picture
  background piece 13
- 2" square of red solid fabric for
  rose pieces 14–19
- 2" x 3" rectangle of mottled
  green fabric for stem
  pieces 20–22
- 4" x 8" rectangle of mottled
  bright yellow fabric for cup and
  teapot pieces 23–28
- 4" x 6" rectangle of mottled
  dark blue fabric for cup and
  teapot pieces 29–30
- 6" x 13" rectangle of mottled
  medium rust fabric for table
  pieces 31–38
- 1¼ yd. fusible web
- 18" x 20" piece of batting
- Black cotton thread for no-sew
  fusible web, plus monofilament
  thread if you use lightweight
  fusible web

CUTTING

From the black solid fabric:

1. Cut 2 strips, each 2½" x 42", for the binding. Set them aside.

2. Cut a 4½" x 16½" rectangle for the hanging sleeve. Set it aside.

3. Cut 2 pieces, each 18" x 20", for the foundation and the quilt backing. For the optional straight-edge border, cut 2 pieces, each 17" x 19". Set them aside.

PREPARING THE APPLIQUÉS

NOTE: *The pattern is the mirror image of your finished quilt. Should you wish to have the finished design face the same direction as the pattern, turn the pattern over and trace the pieces from the backside of the pattern.*

1. You may use either the patterns to create the picture frame that is shown in the photo of this quilt, or you may create a straight-edge border, as shown on all the other projects in this book. If you are making straight borders, draw the border pieces onto the fusible web. Using a ruler, draw two 1" x 15" strips and two 1" x 10½" strips. The 1" x 15" strips will be the top and bottom borders, and the 1" x 10½" strips will be the side borders. If you are making the "pieced" border, skip this step.

2. If you prefer to use the printed patterns to create the border shown in the quilt photograph, refer to page 72 to trace piece A four times, piece B two times, and piece C two times onto your fusible web. Group all of these pieces together because you'll be cutting all of them from the same fabric.

3. Referring to "Tracing the Design onto Fusible Web" on page 7, trace the remaining pattern pieces on pages 69–71 onto your fusible web. Group pieces together that will be cut from the same fabric. For instance, all of the background pieces (1–8) are cut from the mottled peach fabric, so trace them close together on one section of your fusible web. Write the corresponding pattern number on each piece.

4. After you trace all of the pieces, cut the groups apart and fuse them to the wrong side of the appliqué fabrics. Be sure to refer to the manufacturer's instructions for using the fusible web. Cut out each shape and set the appliqués aside.

   You will need to cut out the hole in the spout of the teapot. As an alternative, you may color it in with a black permanent marker or embroider it with black thread.

ASSEMBLING THE QUILT TOP

1. Using a ruler and a marking pencil, measure 2" in from each edge of the foundation fabric and draw a line the full length of each side to use as guidelines. Or see page 8 if you prefer to trace your entire pattern onto the foundation fabric.

2. Referring to the appliqué guide below and the pattern, place the appliqué pieces onto the foundation fabric. Begin with the border strips. If you are making the straight-edge border, place the top and bottom border strips on first. Lay the outside edge of each strip on the drawn line. Next, place the side border strips with their outside edges on the drawn lines. Leave a ¼" gap between the ends of these strips and the edges of the top and bottom strips. Use a ruler to check your spacing if desired.

Appliqué Guide

If you cut your "pieced" border with the templates, draw a second guideline 1½" in from each of the first guidelines. Referring to the border placement diagram, position the corner pieces first with their inner right angles placed along the inside guidelines. Next, place the B pieces on the top and the bottom, and the C pieces on the sides, with their straight edges on the inside guideline. Leave a ¼" gap between the ends of these pieces and the ends of the corner pieces.

3. Continuing to work from the outside edges toward the quilt center, place the remaining appliqué pieces onto the foundation fabric. Leave a ¼" gap between all of the pieces.

NOTE: *There are some exceptions to this rule. Leave only a ⅛" gap between the cup, teapot, and picture frame pieces; leave a ¹/₁₆" gap around and between the roses on these items. Please refer to your pattern for placement guidance.*

4. Once you have all of the pieces in place, stand back and study your quilt top. Make any necessary adjustments. Following the manufacturer's directions for your fusible web, press all of the pieces to adhere them to the foundation. Allow the quilt top to cool.

FINISHING

Refer to "Quilting and Finishing" starting on page 9 to complete your quilt or "Banners" on page 12 to turn your top into a banner.

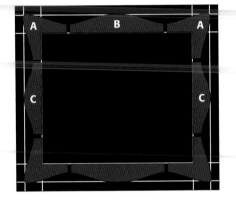

Border placement diagram

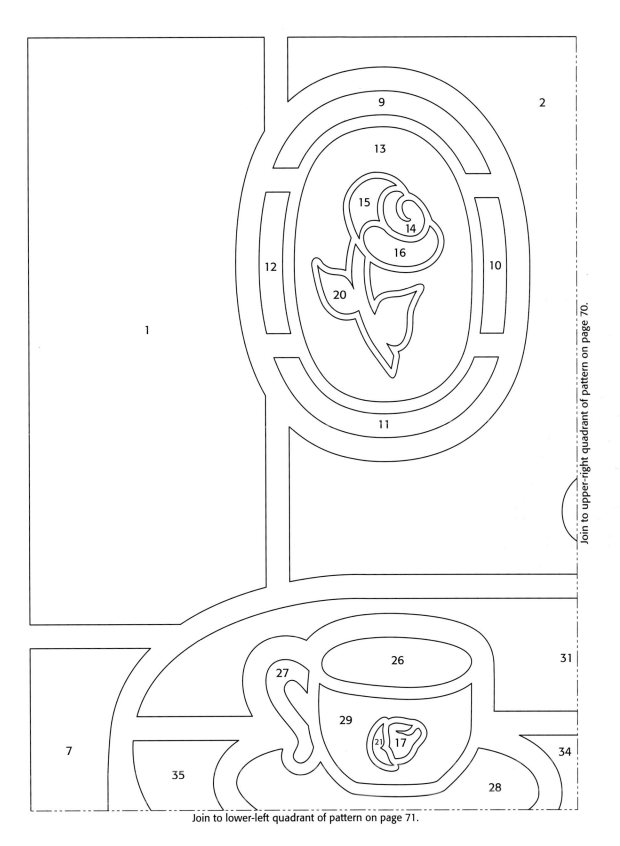

Teatime
Upper-Left Quadrant

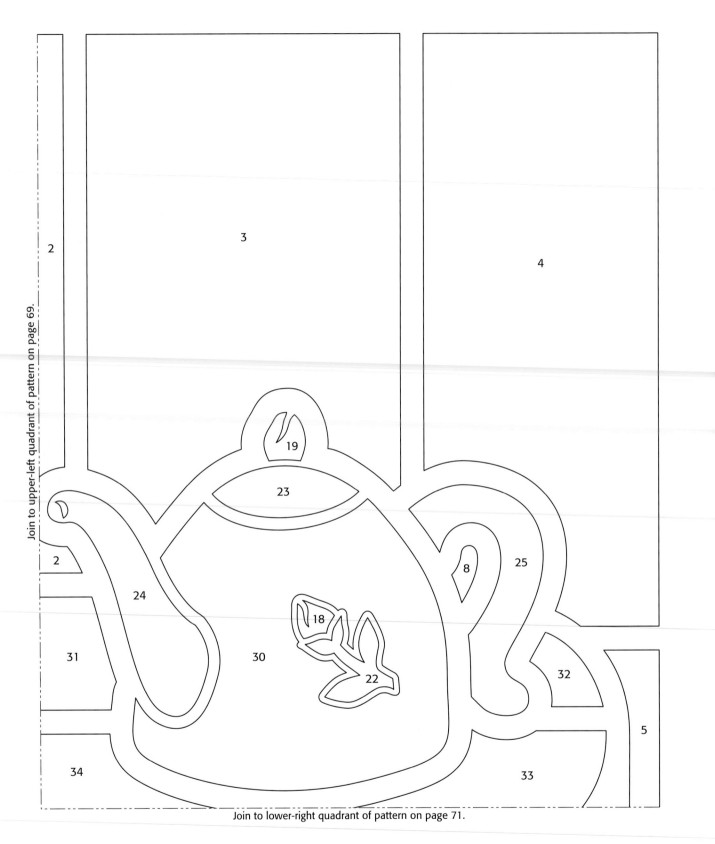

Join to upper-left quadrant of pattern on page 69.

2

3

4

19

23

2

8

25

24

18

31

30

22

32

5

34

33

Join to lower-right quadrant of pattern on page 71.

Teatime
Upper-Right Quadrant

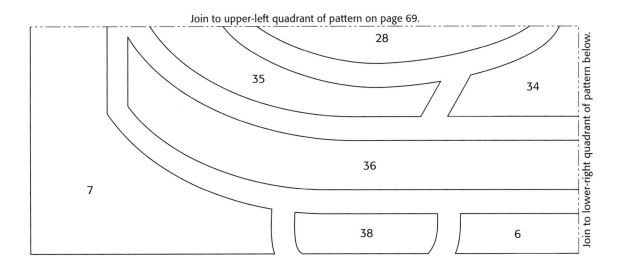

Teatime
Lower-Left Quadrant

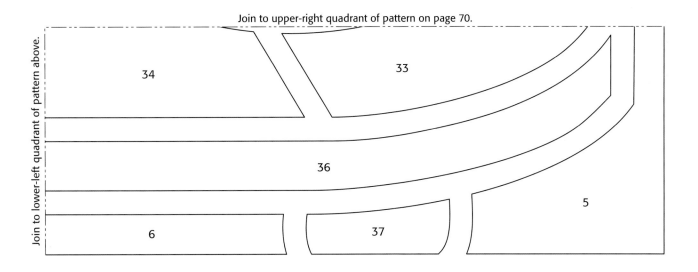

Teatime
Lower-Right Quadrant

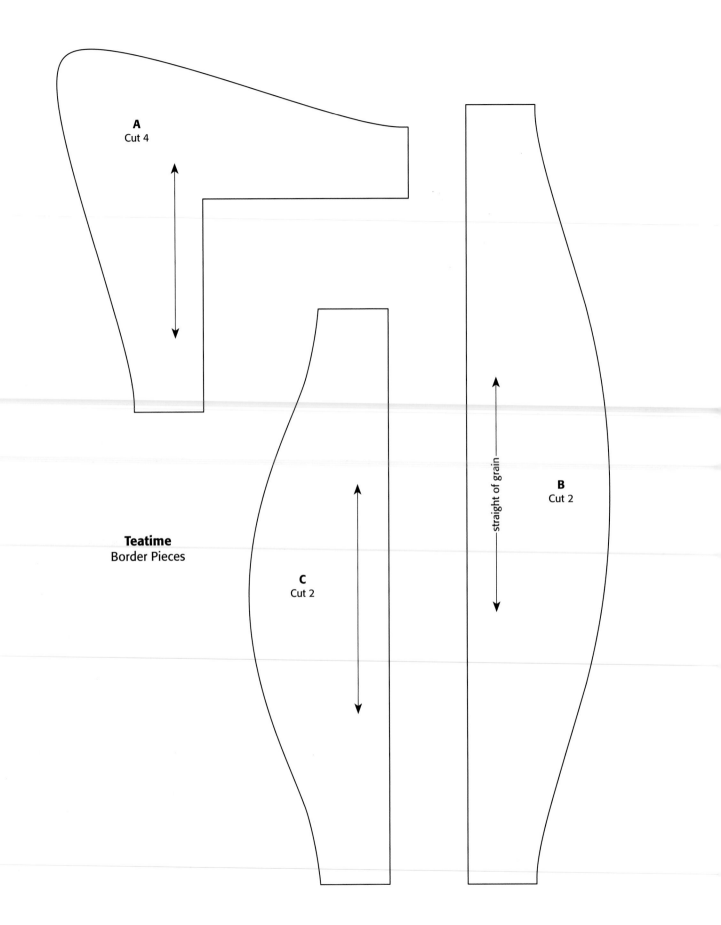

A
Cut 4

B
Cut 2

straight of grain

Teatime
Border Pieces

C
Cut 2

Sitting Pretty by Amy Whalen Helmkamp,
1999, Lake Oswego, Oregon, 16" x 20".

Cats. They sleep, play, give us comfort, and entertain us. And they love to sit and watch all that is happening around them. You might even catch them sitting very prettily, as if posing for a picture.

MATERIALS

All fabrics are 42" wide and 100 percent cotton unless otherwise stated. The following directions are for creating a calico kitty as shown in the photo. Feel free to make your kitty any color you wish. Just choose which colors you want your cat to be and substitute fabrics as you like.

- 1 yd. black solid fabric for foundation, backing, binding, and hanging sleeve
- Fat quarter or 5" x 18" piece of mottled dark purple fabric for border strips
- 18" square of mottled taupe fabric for background pieces 1–8
- 1" x 2" rectangle of light peach fabric for inside ear pieces 9–10
- 8" square of mottled dark brown fabric for cat pieces 11–15
- 5" x 7" rectangle of mottled medium brown fabric for cat pieces 16–18
- 4" x 6" rectangle of mottled cream fabric for cat pieces 19–21
- 4" x 8" rectangle of white print for cat pieces 22–26
- 1" square of light pink fabric for nose piece 27
- 1" x 2" rectangle of yellow-green fabric for eye pieces 28–31
- 4" x 9" rectangle of mottled teal fabric for stool pieces 32–38
- 1 yd. fusible web
- 19" x 23" piece of batting
- Black cotton thread for no-sew fusible web, plus monofilament thread if you use lightweight fusible web

CUTTING

From the black solid fabric:

1. Cut 2 strips, each 2½" x 42", for the binding. Set them aside.

2. Cut a 4½" x 15½" rectangle for the hanging sleeve. Set it aside.

3. Cut 2 pieces, each 19" x 23", for the foundation and the quilt backing. Set them aside.

PREPARING THE APPLIQUÉS

NOTE: *The pattern is the mirror image of your finished quilt. Should you wish to have the finished design face the same direction as the pattern, turn the pattern over and trace the pieces from the backside of the pattern.*

1. Draw the border pieces onto the fusible web. Using a ruler, draw two 1" x 16½" strips and two 1" x 15" strips. The 1" x 16½" strips will be the side borders, and the 1" x 15" strips will be the top and bottom borders.

2. Referring to "Tracing the Design onto Fusible Web" on page 7, trace the pattern pieces on pages 75–78 onto the fusible web. Group pieces together that will be cut from the same fabric. For instance, all of the background pieces (1–8) are cut from the mottled taupe fabric, so trace them close together on one section of your fusible web. Likewise,

group the stool pieces (32–38) together, and so on. Write the corresponding pattern number on each piece.

3. After you trace all of the pieces, cut the groups apart and fuse them to the wrong side of the appliqué fabrics. Be sure to refer to the manufacturer's instructions for using the fusible web. Cut out each shape, and set the appliqués aside.

ASSEMBLING THE QUILT TOP

1. Using a ruler and a marking pencil, measure 2" in from each edge of the foundation fabric and draw a line the full length of each side to use as guidelines. Or see page 8 if you prefer to trace your entire pattern onto the foundation fabric.

2. Referring to the appliqué guide at right and the pattern, place the appliqué pieces onto the foundation fabric. Begin with the border strips. Place the top and bottom border strips on first, laying the outside edge of each strip on the drawn line. Next, place the side border strips with their outside edges on the drawn lines. Leave a ¼" gap between the ends of these strips and the edges of the top and bottom strips. Use a ruler to check your spacing if desired.

Appliqué Guide

3. Continuing to work from the outside edges toward the quilt center, place the remaining appliqué pieces onto the foundation fabric. Leave a ¼" gap between all of the pieces.

   NOTE: *The cat's face is an exception to this rule. Leave only a $^1/_{16}$" gap between these pieces.*

4. Once you have all of the pieces in place, stand back and study your quilt top. Make any necessary adjustments. Following the manufacturer's directions for your fusible web, press all of the pieces to adhere them to the foundation. Allow the quilt top to cool.

FINISHING

Refer to "Quilting and Finishing" starting on page 9 to complete your quilt or "Banners" on page 12 to turn your top into a banner.

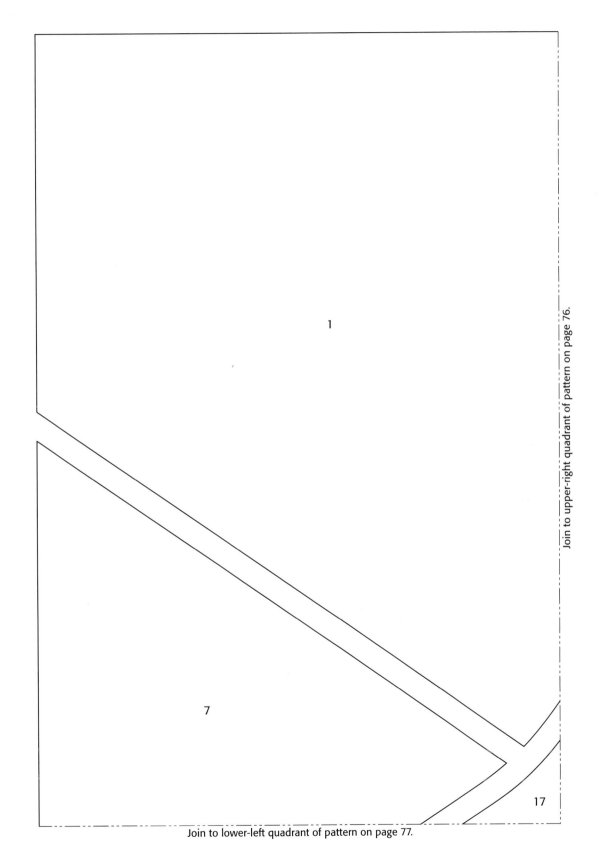

Join to upper-right quadrant of pattern on page 76.

1

7

17

Join to lower-left quadrant of pattern on page 77.

Sitting Pretty
Upper-Left Quadrant

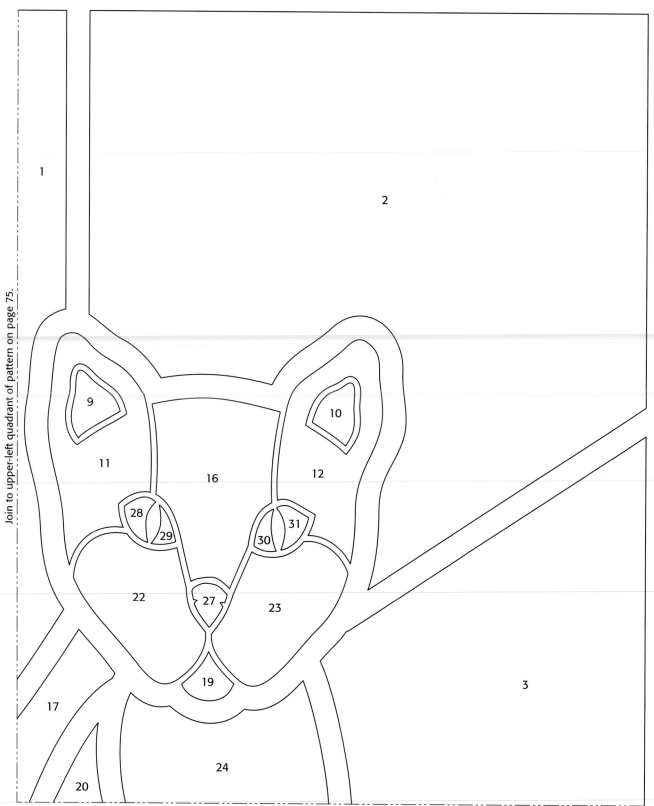

Join to upper-left quadrant of pattern on page 75.

Join to lower-right quadrant of pattern on page 78.

Sitting Pretty
Upper-Right Quadrant

Join to upper-left quadrant of pattern on page 75.

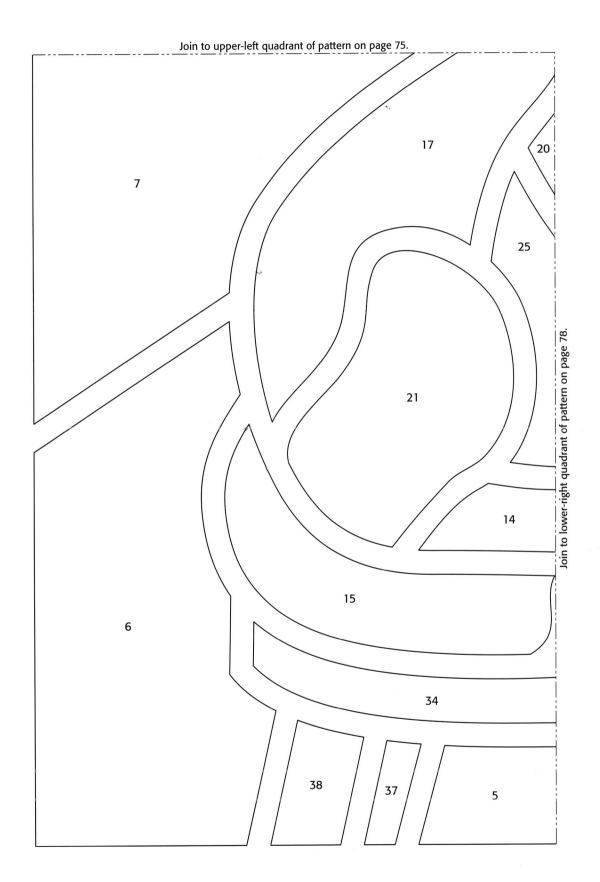

Join to lower-right quadrant of pattern on page 78.

Sitting Pretty
Lower-Left Quadrant

Join to upper-right quadrant of pattern on page 76.

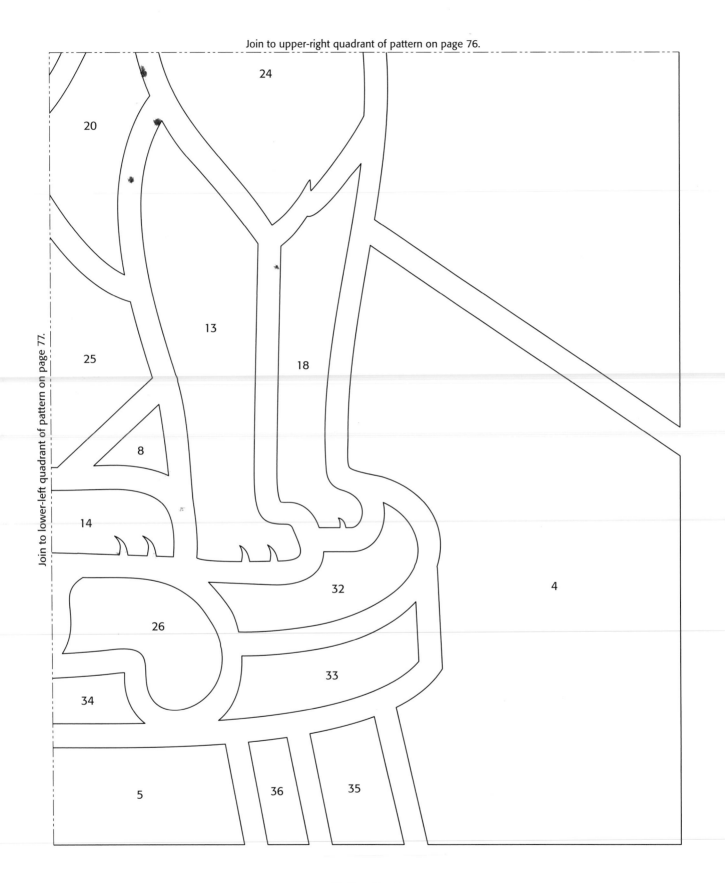

Join to lower-left quadrant of pattern on page 77.

Sitting Pretty
Lower-Right Quadrant